W9-AMQ-605

Harbors of Enchantment

A YACHTSMAN'S ANTHOLOGY

By Cynthia Kaul

with Jill Bobrow and Dana Jinkins

DANA JINKINS

Harbors of Enchantment

A YACHTSMAN'S ANTHOLOGY

By Cynthia Kaul

with Jill Bobrow and Dana Jinkins

CONCEPTS
PUBLISHING INC.

DANA JINKINS

This book is dedicated to my parents, Tom and Bette,
who inspired me with their love of life and journeys.

Third Edition 1995

Library of Congress Cataloging-in-Publication Data

Kaul, Cynthia C., 1951-
Harbors of Enchantment...a yachtsman's anthology.

1. Yachts and yachting. 2. Harbors. I. Title.
GV813.K34 1989 387.1 89-15700
ISBN 0-393-02761-9

Concepts Publishing Inc.
P.O. Box 1066
Bridge Street Marketplace
Waitsfield, Vermont 05673
Telephone: 802 496-5580
Facsimile: 802 496-5581
Telex: 4949444 BOOKS

Distributed by:
W.W. Norton & Company, Inc.
500 Fifth Avenue, New York, N.Y. 10110

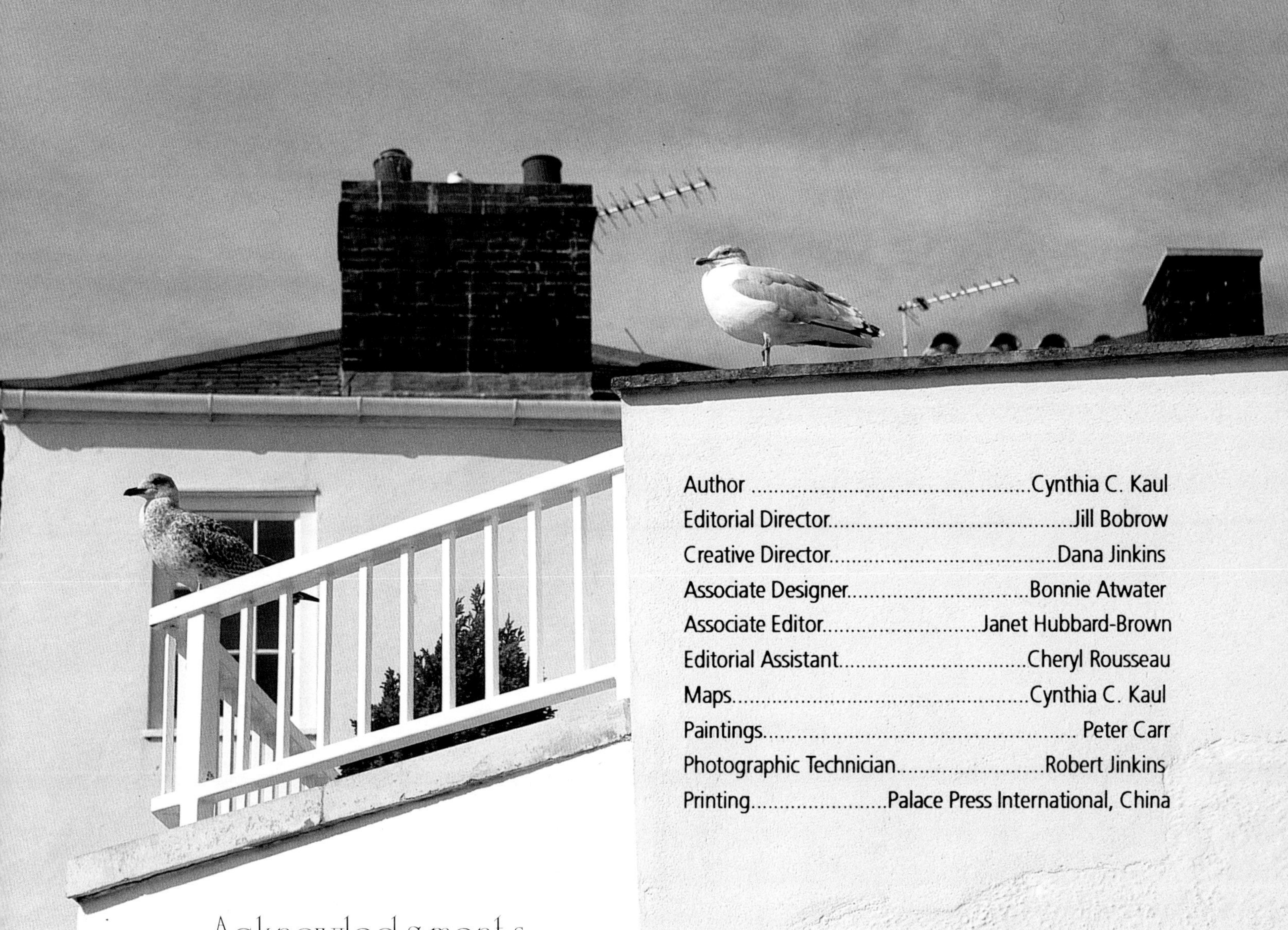

Author ....Cynthia C. Kaul
Editorial Director.......................................Jill Bobrow
Creative Director.......................................Dana Jinkins
Associate Designer.................................Bonnie Atwater
Associate Editor..............................Janet Hubbard-Brown
Editorial Assistant..................................Cheryl Rousseau
Maps..Cynthia C. Kaul
Paintings...Peter Carr
Photographic Technician..........................Robert Jinkins
Printing.......................Palace Press International, China

Acknowledgments

Many people contributed their energy and resources to the creation of this book. I am most grateful to Jill Bobrow and Dana Jinkins who persisted in harnessing me to this project. I truly appreciate their confidence, encouragement and support throughout. I wish to thank my editors, Jill Bobrow and Janet Hubbard-Brown, who helped immensely to groom my text and generously pitched in with words and ideas when my inspiration was flagging. I also wish to thank Bill Stedman and Keith Anderson who contributed their insights and good judgement to the editorial process. Along the way, my life's course and interests have been influenced by my seafaring friends. I would like to convey my greetings and gratitude to them.

Jill, Dana and I would like to express our gratitude to a number of people whose experience, logs and comments assisted in compiling information for this book: Robin Taylor, James Andrews, and June Field for their valuable assistance in England. Alison Langley, Herb Kiendl, Neil Rabinowitz, Preben Nyeland, Roe Anne White, Mike Beale, Jeannette Phillipps, Mark Padbury, Nicola and Peter Dent, Barry Bailey, John Donovan, Bill Nowlan, Klaus Alvermann, Reid Stowe, Patricia Dent, Kenny Mitchnick, Johnny Summers, Marty Jinkins, Matthew Toth, Nicole Perraud, Mattey and Paula DeWijs, Stanton Parks, Natalie Guillaume, Alanna Fagan, Bill Cannell and B'fer Burton. And we are most grateful to all the correspondents whose letters are included throughout the book.

We wish to thank Bonnie Atwater for her indefatigability and creative design assistance, and Jim Edgcomb and Jeff Schoellkopf of Edgcomb Design Group for computer assistance and support. Also we want to thank David, Gene and Don at Maya Computer and Mark at Wordgraphics for their technical assistance. We thank Jim Mairs, Eric Swenson and Bill Rusen of W.W. Norton & Co., Inc., who have consistently supported our efforts at Concepts Publishing.

We couldn't have produced the book without the many photographers who contributed their excellent work, and wish to thank all of them. We appreciate Bob Jinkins and David Garten for their darkroom assistance and Cheryl Rousseau for her cheerfulness and office organization.

☆ Maps are not to be used for navigation.

☆ Appendix of photographers in the back of the book represents those who contributed a significant number of photographs.

☆ Harbors is sometimes spelled Harbours (or as our British friends think **vice versa**). Letters written in this book by various people have been left with the individual's spelling of Harbors/Harbours intact.

Contents

DANA JINKINS

DANA JINKINS

DANA JINKINS

Preface

My early horizons were lengthened by my first glimpse of Russian ships in the port of Duluth and the possibilities that harkened along the St. Lawrence seaway. The vision sired my unending quest for foreign shores. We all met, Jill, Dana and I as well as most of our contributing correspondents — on the shores of an enchanting harbor. What we had in common has been described by Nantucket photographer, Eric Pawley,

"While it varies with characteristic charm and delight of each port, the essence of what attracts us to harbors follows a track in every sailor's memory and place-love. The old story of our two great pleasures of sailing — departing the harbor, and returning, is programmed in us like sunrise and sunset, the joy of morning and the gratefulness of bed at night. The lovely Arabic name of the East African port Dar-es Salaam (Haven of Peace), tucked in behind Zanzibar, and our own Harbor of Refuge, at Point Judith, are witness to this love affair with place."

We have attempted to bring to this book our cumulative knowledge and impressions of the various ports of call we have entered, reveling in the quiet beauty and haiku spareness of deserted anchorages and the cultural excitement and clamor of larger ports.

Traditional harborfronts encircled by noise, commotion and dirty, railroady warehouse zones were purlieus of passion and intrigue. The air was infused with the tongues of faraway places and the careless exuberance of sailors on shore leave. Itinerants among us know the release — and the strong appetites — cultivated by privations and exertions at sea. In many countries these harbors now cater to a different trade. The wharves no longer store and ship bulk cargo and containerized shipment has obviated the need for large crews. Restoration and gentrification of urban centers has done a lot to change these harbors. Without the noise and ruckus and forbidden fruit, the waterfront has been restored to the public, who still savor the thrill of it all.

We wish to present this survey of enchanting harbors in a spirit of respect and with a desire to retain their allure.

We invite our readers to embark with us on an imaginary cruising route from the Pacific Coast of America, west around the world, with detours and delays and allowances for seasons. This perusal of harbors, anchorages and other waterside attractions does not aspire to be a cruising guide, but rather an anthology of nautical life. Whether you are a venerable "old salt," an armchair voyager, or are about to take your first cruise, I hope this book provides a porthole to some of the world's most enchanting harbors.

Cynthia C Kraul

Introduction

The community of cruising sailors is a unique clique — international and peripatetic. There are the 'round the world cruising sailors who keep bumping into each other in remote islands of the South Pacific. Then again, there is the close-knit charterboat clan which bounces biannually from port to port in New England, the Caribbean and the Mediterranean — and the racing nuts who meet regularly in places like Newport, Porto Cervo, Falmouth or Perth — but mostly there are your run-of-the-mill sea gypsies who show up almost any place you find water and boats. The sea is the common bond and harbors are what bring this diverse cast of characters together.

Bequia in the Grenadines is where Dana Jinkins and I met. Some of our closest friendships were developed in the West Indies, including Cynthia Kaul, author of this book. We all left Bequia, and Dana and I started a publishing company. Cynthia kept in touch through prolific letters. We savored her stories, images, and textured descriptions. We determined that she was a natural to write this book.

But Cynthia has many interests; it was hard to lassoo her and bring her into an office environment where she had to sit at a computer. She stared out the window a lot and grumbled about the fluorescent flu and the lack of oxygen. Cynthia likes to make up words and our associate editor, Janet, would have conniption fits over "fabularies of statuaries" and too many commas. I felt like "Le Petit Prince" trying to domesticate a wild thing — I only hope we left in enough of the poetry.

This account is not only the world according to Cynthia and us, but also as seen through the eyes of innumerable correspondents and photographers. The paintings interspersed throughout the book were taken from the journals of our itinerent Australian friend Peter Carr, an inveterate sailor who cruises and races with the best of them. It's impossible to stroll down a dock anywhere without hearing him say "G'day mate" to a half dozen of his closest friends.

This book was a challenge for Dana and me. Even though we personally produced our previous three books, the scope of this project was more overwhelming. I was on the phone, fax and telex constantly trying to find sources for photos and testimonials. Dana had the enormous challenge of having to coordinate a zillion photographs and edit them to represent the world plus match the voluminous text to the appropriate pages containing those photographs. The most monumental hurdle was the fact that Dana, who heretofore had always been computer-resistant, decided to try and design this whole book on a Macintosh! Add a learning curve to a 288-page-book with a near impossible deadline and you have the kind of stress that is totally non-existent in those enchanting harbors whereof we speak!

Jill Bobrow

DANA JINKINS

DANA JINKINS

DANA JINKINS

PACIFIC NORTHWEST

BRITISH COLUMBIA

The lacework of islands and peninsulas continues in lovely quiet splendor along mainland British Columbia and Vancouver Island. Immense waterfalls and glaciers are born of the sawtooth coastal range. Intricate inlets offer boundless cruising possibilities, abundant seafood, freshwater lakes and ample attractions ashore. It is a land of incomparable beauty.

At the northern end of the Strait of Georgia is Desolation Sound, the Discovery Islands and the maze of Bute Inlet. Much of this area has been designated as a provincial marine park.

Remnants of logging and Indian settlements provide interesting discoveries. There is excellent hiking and swimming at Malaspina Inlet. Petroglyphs and pictographs can be perused in Manson's Landing on Cortes Island.

Squirrel Cove is another great anchorage. Tucked behind a hidden entrance is a large cove containing a cluster of islands and bays. One inlet connects via tidal rapids to a still lagoon where the water is warm and the intertidal fauna are a wonder to float over and behold. It's like a kayak course for dinghies that you might share with otters. Outside the cove is a colorful Indian village. Oysters, salmon, mussels and clams are plentiful in these waters.

PRINCESS LOUISA INLET

The most extravagant mountain scenery on the coast rewards the voyager to Princess Louisa Inlet. Boats must travel 40 miles up the fjord of Jervis Inlet to Malibu Rapids, then wait for slack water to transit the tidal rapids and proceed on into Princess Louisa. It's hard to imagine anything grander than the breathtaking pageant of sheer cliffs, 200-foot falls and pictographs comprising Princess Louisa Inlet. You can even swim alongside glaciers. Anchorage is possible at Princess Louisa Marine Park, under the roaring spectacle of the Chatterbox Falls.

NEIL RABINOWITZ

C.

In many ways, Princess Louisa in British Columbia is the ultimate gunkhole, the dramatic dead-end of a thousand-foot-deep fjord off Desolation Sound. Cruising there is more of a backpack than a voyage. As the snow-capped mountains close in, glaciers can be seen sparkling in the sun. Finally, the mountains crowd to the water and there is the narrow entrance looking for all the world like a white-water kayak course.

Once inside, you cruise for several miles in a land-locked pristine wilderness before reaching the anchorage at the foot of a breathtaking waterfall that cascades down the rocky slopes for hundreds of feet. At sunset, bears amble down to the beach unmindful of the boat anchored several hundred feet away. The rocks are covered with oysters. The air is moist and redolent with pine. For me, Princess Louisa is a two-word synonym for paradise.

Oliver S. Moore III
Publisher/ Yachting Magazine

NEIL RABINOWITZ

A.

B.

DEBORAH MACNEIL

VANCOUVER & VICTORIA

The Strait of Georgia continues in a panorama of snow-capped alps for 100 miles to the Gulf and San Juan Islands, and down to the cosmopolitan feast of Vancouver.

False Creek in downtown Vancouver Harbor offers convenient marinas and walking access to the city lights and restaurants. Gastown and Chinatown are two distinctive waterfront neighborhoods with culinary and ethnic pizazz. The anthropological museum on the University of British Columbia campus is superb and also handy to False Creek. Stanley Park, a peninsular preserve in the harbor with majestic stands of spruce and huge western red cedar, is a pleasant vantage point for harbor viewing.

Vancouver (formerly Granville and "Gastown") is scarcely 100 years old. The railway engendered the first boom, while shipping was growing apace. The seaport is currently experiencing a renewed commercial importance in the Pacific Basin. A nexus for exquisite cruising destinations, it is also an interesting urban hiatus.

And then there is groomed and gardened British Victoria, the provincial capital on Vancouver Island. This well-protected harbor has several mooring choices, and is scaled more appropriately to small craft. The Parliament buildings and the Empress Hotel frame the inner harbor. It is a comely city, full of blossoms, and accessible by bike or dinghy. The art scene is as lively in Victoria as in Vancouver, and the Provincial Museum here is excellent.

A. Parliament buildings at Victoria
B. False Creek, Vancouver
C. Downtown Vancouver
D. Roche Harbor, San Juan Islands, Washington
E. Anchorage in San Juan Islands

THE SAN JUAN ISLANDS

Supposedly the notorious "wet coast" lets up a bit in the area around Victoria, the Gulf Islands and the San Juans. Sun shines on this gorgeous cruising area even when fog besets the Olympic Peninsula and rain falls on Seattle. This evergreen archipelago is lush and lovely, and alive with fauna.

The San Juan Islands are comprised of approximately 200 islands in the Strait of Juan de Fuca; here the American continent meets the Pacific and Canada meets the United States. They include the full spectrum of anchorages. Roche Harbor is a San Juan "hotspot," where snippets of history — a former boom-town hotel and a Hudson's Bay post dating from 1886 — have been gussied up to become a swank resort with beautiful gardens and marina.

The San Juans include quiet anchorages like the lagoon in Fisherman Bay on Lopez Island, which has a hair-raising serpentine entrance before opening out into pastoral serenity. The fishing port of Mackaye Harbor, with its old inn and fresh-baked goods at Richardson's General Store, is another peaceful anchorage; excellent abalone diving is nearby.

The Matia and Sucia Islands are marine parks that also offer exceptional diving. This reefy little archipelago has marine fossils, caves and pillars of rock. In the anchorage at Echo Bay, sun dapples swimmers in a pristine cove garlanded with pines. In the distance, the ethereal spectre of Mt. Baker's peak looms above a hazy cloud of moisture which obscures its base.

TONY L. HOTSKY

C.

BARRY BAILEY

D.

E.

NEIL RABINOWITZ

NEIL RABINOWITZ

B.

NEIL RABINOWITZ

PUGET SOUND

British explorer Vancouver named Whidbey Island after his mate of the same name, who discovered the narrow pass which separates it from the mainland. Having navigated under the misconception that it was a peninsula, he called the steep-walled cut Deception Pass. This cut issues from the tempestuous Strait of Juan de Fuca into the protected channel of Puget Sound.

Port Townsend on the Quimper Peninsula, next to Olympic National Park, is the original harbor at this strategic junction of waters. It fell from prominence last century when the railroad located its terminus at Seattle, but it remains a quaint and handsome town with a large fleet of fishing and pleasure craft and a thriving trade in wooden boatbuilding.

Penn Cove on Whidbey Island was a grain port 100 years ago, reputedly accessible on any tide. Historic Coupeville Wharf in Penn Cove has been restored with yacht facilities and is a good base for browsing in the antique stores or for setting off on cycling tours around the island. It is a rolling, bucolic island with fields and clusters of arbutus, an unusual evergreen which keeps its glossy green leaves, but sheds its bark to reveal bright orange wood.

Puget Sound offers many alternatives for cruising in relative degrees of civilization — Bainbridge, Vashon, Blake Island, Budd Inlet, Hood Canal are some of them — but one of the outstanding spectacles is the harbor of Seattle! Ships and tugs are constantly plying the bay against the backdrop of an imposing, beautiful city. For more scenic enjoyment, you can take the Lake Washington Ship Canal through the Chittenden Locks and climb with the salmon to Lake Washington. The long lake is surrounded with scenic terraces of houses on hilly slopes. Twilight can be delicious, anchored in the lee of Sand Point Park. As the sun sets on rosy Mt. Rainier, reflections fade and are replaced by city lights.

A. Montlake cut through Seattle
B. Wooden Boat Festival, Port Townsend
C. Mt. Baker off Whidbey Island
D. Yacht construction, Port Townsend

NEIL RABINOWITZ

C.

NEIL RABINOWITZ

D.

Port Townsend was saved from progress by Seattle. As the first truly protected deep water port inside the Strait of Juan de Fuca, it was intended to become the Northwest metropolis. Ships arrived from throughout the world hauling lumber off the Olympic Peninsula and sea captains built grand Victorian homes on the hillsides overlooking the harbor. But the railway never crossed Puget Sound, and instead, a small port east of the Sound became the rail terminus. They named it after an old Indian Chief Sealth and called it Seattle. Port Townsend, which for years was the busiest city north of San Francisco, decided to sulk in history, resisting change and development. It still is an anachronistic port where traditional shipbuilders teach the classic trades of wooden boat construction. The Northwest School of Wooden Boatbuilding is actively training craftsmen of the future, preserving a maritime art.

Once each year history comes alive in this sleepy port which has served as guardian over Puget Sound for more than a century. The Port Townsend Wooden Boat Festival has been thriving for a decade as one of the country's liveliest boating festivals.

Besides their jamboree of wooden boats, the town itself is always alive with salty characters who think of their tiny town as a mecca for traditional sailors. During the festival, week-long workshops and seminars are led by expert craftsmen. Wooden boats from 7-150 feet long, line the docks in one of the town's harbors. Sea stories are swapped up and down the waterfront and proud owners, sailors and other dreamers mingle on the dock, unconsciously fondling some rounded turn of teak.

In summer, Port Townsend is an offbeat retreat that offers the Hot Jazz Festival, a Fiddle Festival, a Kayak symposium that brings kayakers from throughout the country and the Classic Mariner Regatta, a hot-blooded competition among some of the nations traditional yachts.

Neil Rabinowitz
Photographer
Bainbridge Island, WA

NEIL RABINOWITZ

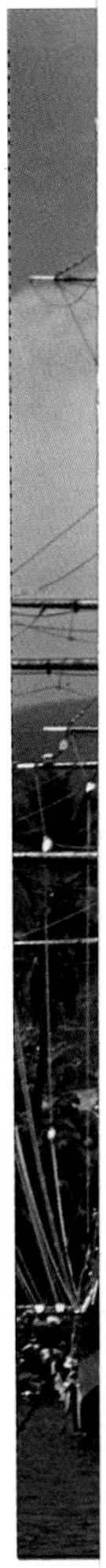

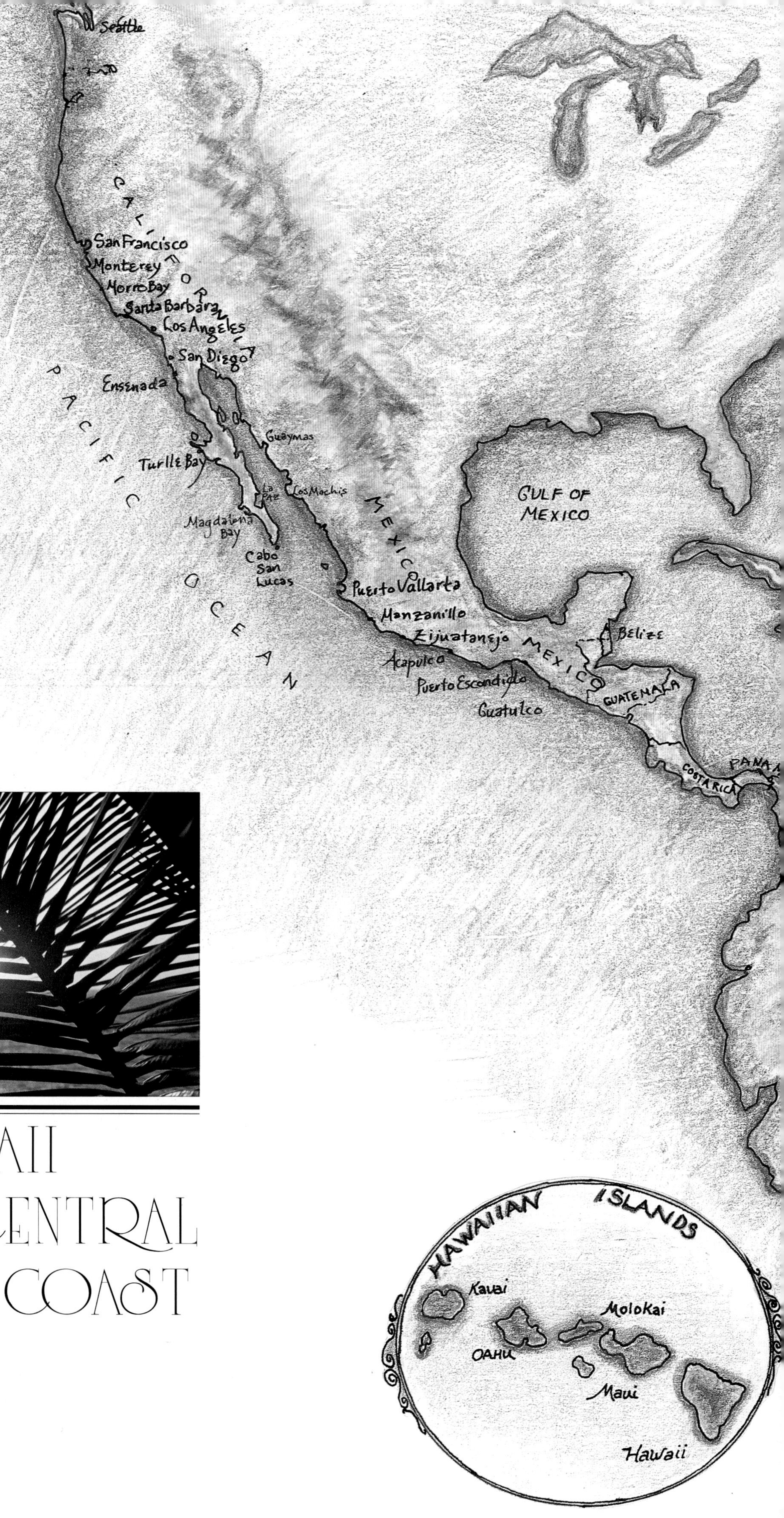

ROBERT JINKINS

HAWAII & THE CENTRAL PACIFIC COAST

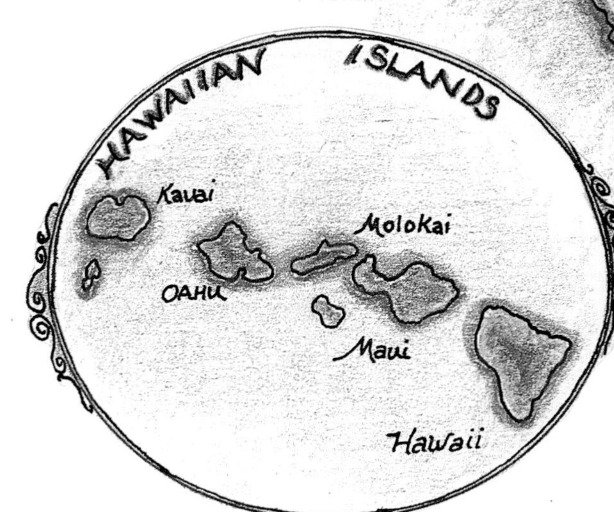

RICK MALOOF

A.

RICK MALOOF

B.

vibrant tapestry. The most visible signs of this culture are not, however, on the coasts. Mexican ports on the Pacific tend to be sleepy, sunny havens of fishermen and campesinos, with palm-thatched *palapas* and *cantinas* pitched along the beach.

Zijuatanejo, on a lovely bay shaded by palms and blessed with beaches, was a village of this ilk. One of the beaches, Ixtapa, has been developed and descended upon in a big way by the package tours from the north land and Mexico City.

Acapulco Bay is the finest natural harbor on the coast. Its natural splendor was discovered long ago and its sloping shores and cliff tops have been growing glamorous appendages and high-rise hotels for decades. It is still a striking spectacle from seaward as well as inside. The Acapulco Yacht Club is a welcome oasis away from the hubbub.

Down the coast, Puerto Escondido provides a glimpse of what Acapulco used to be. This port is a locus for cruising yachts, artists and travelers, and has a casual cosmopolitan appeal. South of here, Puerto Angel and Guatulco offer shelter and a disheveled sort of charm.

COSTA RICA

Costa Rica is an interesting country with a different and more peaceful history than the rest of strife-torn Central America. There are several good anchorages along the coast. Punta Arenas in the Gulf of Nicoya is a busy port on a sand spit where yachts usually clear customs and provision. There are preferable alternatives in the islands and inlets of this large gulf. Hacienda Nicoya is a quiet little spot with a *palapa* restaurant and volleyball games. Golfito is another pleasant port farther south, near the Panamanian border. Yachts congregate at an anchorage a few miles to the north of the banana pier, near a popular watering hole, Captain Tom's. Captain Tom, a one-legged United States expatriate, presides over this genial compound.

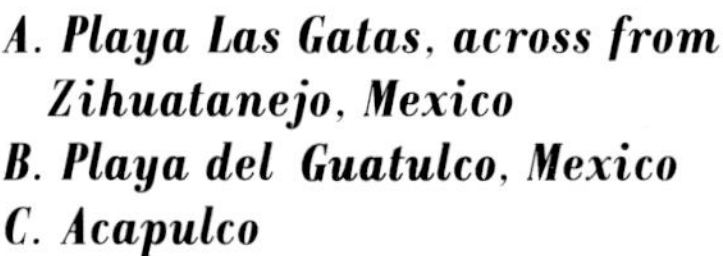

A. Playa Las Gatas, across from Zihuatanejo, Mexico
B. Playa del Guatulco, Mexico
C. Acapulco
D. E. Puerto Viejo, Costa Rica

ROE ANNE WHITE

C. D.

RICK MALOOF

E.

RICK MALOOF

SOUTH PACIFIC

RA Island
CHRISTMAS Island
SOLOMON ISLANDS
ELLICE ISLANDS
SAMOA ISLANDS
Apia
Pago Pago
VANUATU
ESPIRITO SANTO
MALAKULA
Yasawas
Taveuni
Suva
FIJI
LAU GROUP
Va'vau Group
Nius
TONGA
Ha'apai Group
NEW CALEDONIA
TUAM
Bora Bora
Maupiti
Huahine
Moorea
Tahiti
SOCIETY ISLANDS
Rarotonga
COOK ISLANDS
NEW ZEALAND

NORTH
AMERICA
GALAPAGOS
ISLANDS
ARQUESAS
ISLANDS
FATU HIVA
RCHIPELAGO
Easter Island
SOUTH
AMERICA
THE
PACIFIC OCEAN

CYNTHIA SPIRITI
A.

CYNTHIA SPIRITI
B.

C.

CYNTHIA SPIRITI

PALMYRA

Flourishing just north of the equator is the lush, uninhabited island of Palmyra, which is actually a lagoon sheltered by several coral atolls. Remnants of U.S. installations there are quickly reverting to jungle. A letter from one American cruising sailor, Cynthia Spiriti, describes the scene as follows: *One building has been taken over by visiting sailors and playfully referred to as the Palmyra Yacht Club. Here one sees the artwork of the few who pass this way. Paintings of yachts, or at least names, cover every beam and wall. The airstrip has been claimed by thousands of terns where they nest and teach their young to fly. Boobies nest along the beaches, and fairy terns flutter silently overhead. There are two full time residents, "Palmyra" and "Army", who subside on roots and small sharks. Often we awoke to find them in our dinghy. They are dogs.*

NIUE

Niue is an unusual little island on the route to Tonga, an uplifted coral plateau with a reef around it. Anchorage is in fairly deep, crystal clear water on a shelf off the village of Alofi. The coast on the lee side here is a wall of cliffs with deep chasms and caves full of prehistory. In contrast, the windward side has dramatic rainforests.

One hundred feet up is the village of Alofi, sparsely populated with friendly, curious people. Alofi is tidy and cheerful, and welcoming to rare visitors. Exploring about, though, the place feels somewhat deserted. It is a province of New Zealand, and much of the population is over there for years at a time earning a living. Many of the houses stand empty waiting for the people to return. Those that stay make beautiful, intricate basketry.

A.B.C. Palmyra - Beach, Bathtub, Yacht Club
D. Girl from Taveuni village
E. Huahine, Society Islands
F. Boat boys

SAMOA

Despite a century of interference from foreigners, the people of western Samoa retain more of their traditional Polynesian values and customs than people elsewhere in Oceania. Land is owned communally by family groups, headed by an elected *matai*, who is responsible for everyone's well being. The Samoans live in round huts without walls, sharing most meals and chores.

The island of Apia Upolu was discovered in its native state by Robert Louis Stevenson in 1890. Sailing around these islands he found himself intrigued by the primitive culture. He had always been plagued by poor respiratory health and eventually settled at Apia, and in this salubrious climate he lived happily and achieved great works. His grave lies on a mountain top here with his famous epitaph,

Under the wide and starry sky,
Dig the grave and let me lie.
Glad did I live and gladly die,
And I laid me down with a will.

This be the verse you grave for me:
Here he lies where he longed to be:
Home is the sailor, home from the sea,
And the hunter home from the hill.

The neighboring island of American Samoa is a different story. It is a sorry illustration of what happens when a materialistic culture is grafted onto a communal island society. The wonderful natural harbor of Pago Pago was the impetus for American interest there in the late last century. It served as a naval base until strategic quarters moved nearer Asia. Large canneries based here catch and process the greater part of all tuna caught in the South Pacific.

These days American Samoa is a welfare state, rather reluctantly self-governing. With home rule, American Samoa ended decades of U.S. funding, which, along with consumer products from abroad, created a totally unrealistic, artificial standard of living.

ALISON LANGLEY

D.

STEPHANIE BERKE

E.

F.

STEPHANIE BERKE

STEPHANIE BERKE

A.

TONGA

The Kingdom of Tonga is the first to welcome each new day. Located just west of the International dateline, this remarkable small nation is the only Pacific nation never to come under foreign rule. In the 13th century Tongan sovreignty extended all the way to Hawaii. The physical stature of its people is uncommonly large. The last monarchy is friendly and still very tradition-bound.

The royal succession of Tongan kings has been recorded by the locals for a thousand years. Queen Salote, six feet tall, ruled Tonga from 1918 until 1965. She was succeeded by her son, King Taufa'ahau Tupou IV. The King's birthday, the 4th of July, is a big national festival in the kingdom, and some sailing friends had the good fortune to take part in his birthday ceremony in the Va'vau group. This happened to be the first year that the ceremony took place in that island group. Herb Kiendl from the yacht *Show Me* described the spectacle in a letter excerpted here.

The tapa cloth is one of the many fine crafts indigenous to Tonga. The bark of the paper mulberry tree is stripped and beaten with rubber mallets, and then dyed and painted in sepia and black tones. This article is traditionally used to sit on, to cover the walls, and to wear as ceremonial dress.

Captain Cook visited Tonga in the 1770s, and got a friendly reception. He presented a gift of a male Galapagos turtle, who wandered for 200 years in the royal garden at Tongatapu until he died in 1966.

It was an incredible show! All boats in attendance, including some French and Australian military vessels, as well as 50 or 60 yachts, were tied up stern-to on the sloping shore of the town side, for the king to review the fleet. Along he came, seated in majesterial splendor atop a throne on a smallish motor boat...all 7 feet and 300 and some pounds of him. The King is in his 60's.

Then the races of long canoes took place, powered by 20 paddlers each and grandly festooned with palms and flowers. The afternoon ensued with more competitive games and a feast. In an underground "umu", 500 pigs were roasted as well as enough fish and paw paw and yams, etc., for the multitude gathered, including the visiting sailors. It was like sitting down before a great mountain of food for each guest; fish, coconuts, yams and breadfruit, with the whole pig in the middle of it. Mind you, an ample girth is a sign of wealth, beauty and stature in this society, and if anyone is watching his figure, he is smiling as he watches it protrude. When all were sated, the villagers lifted the tables, like stretchers, still full of the annual offering from the king, and took it home to their village where they feasted for several days more.

We carried on in our journey, making a spectacular stop in a marginal anchorage, under the volcano on the island of Tofua in the Ha'apai Group. Gases and flames still emerge from the caldera, with all of this going on we actually went swimming with whales. It was here that Fletcher Christian set Captain Bligh and crew adrift to seek their destiny in an open boat. The mutiny victims received a murderous welcome on Tofua, and so pushed off for a journey of 6500 kilometers to Timor.

Herb Kiendl

Herb Kiendl
American Professional Yacht Skipper

FIJI

The Fiji island group is horseshoe shaped, with Viti Levu and Yasawa to the west, Vanua Levu to the north, and the Lau group to the east. They encircle the Koro Sea containing a sprinkling of smaller islands. The entire archipelago is laced with reefs, which are more noteworthy for their diving excellence than their menace to the mariner.

Suva Harbor, on Vanua Levu, is the main dispatch and commercial port in the South Pacific. It is on the weather side of a very rainy island, and has an entrance fraught with reefs. The yacht club here is friendly, however, and there is access to all manner of chandlers and supplies.

On the sunny side of Vanua Levu is Lautoka. There is a wonderful market here where boats often provision for a trip out into the Yasawas, which offer unlimited possibilities for isolated cruising and great diving. A fleet of large catamarans has opened this circuit to the public.

There are a myriad of caves to snorkel and dive on in the Yasawas. Also in this archipelago is Musket Cove on Mololailai, which is a gathering point for many cruising boats. A resort and yacht club sponsors an annual regatta in mid-September. Malololailai is a cruising mecca, as well as a point of divergence for sailors. From here they proceed south to New Zealand, west to New Caledonia and Vanuatu, or north-east to America.

Perhaps the most friendly and magnificent island in all of Fiji is Taveuni. Its high spine to the Pacific brings it abundant rainfall which engenders a wild garden of luxuriant growth, making it home for a great variety of bird life. The stalwart can make a memorable hike to a crater lake at 900 meters. Waterfalls abound in the rainforest, the most noteworthy being Mbouma Falls.

A. Neiafu, Vava'u Islands
B. Waterslide on Taveuni
C. Booma Village, Taveuni

ALISON LANGLEY

B.

C.

ALISON LANGLEY

STEPHANIE BERKE

A.

B.

ALISON LANGLEY

After weeks of negotiating with the Fijian bureaucracy we were finally issued a permit to visit Fulanga in the Lau group - the highlight of our voyaging in 1988. There one only finds traditional, indigenous Fijians. It would be difficult to find a more delightful people. During our three week visit we were treated to three 'mekes' (feasts), with dancing, singing, and gift-giving. Each 'meke' was used as an occasion to raise money for the church, and we were pleased to make generous contributions.

Fulanga is unique in that the atoll is made of limestone instead of coral, and the sparkling, jade green lagoon is dotted with several hundred small mushroom shaped islets. It is the home of the traditional wood carvers and builders of sailing outrigger canoes. These are the last sailors in Fiji, having decided several years ago to eschew the outboard motor that is ubiquitous elsewhere. Sailing canoes are much more practical for everyday use as fuel and parts for outboards are expensive and difficult to obtain.

A number of the young men in the village were commissioned to carve some classic war clubs and table implements under the tutelage of one of the village leaders. They faithfully reproduced exquisite works of art precisely to the dimensions and details illustrated in the catalogue I found in the Suva museum.

We were overwhemed by the genuine hospitality and friendliness of the Fulangans. Although their life is basic and functions at subsistence level, most are educated and speak English. All of the children go to school, but there were hardly any books for them or the adults to read. As a souvenir of our appreciation we contributed an English Library fund to the island.

Marguerite Johnstone,
American Yacht owner, S/Y *Asteroid*

Cruising in the independent kingdom of Tonga and Fiji is different from the other island groups in Oceania. Each island is owned by someone, a chief who must be approached with decorum and *kava* by the master of the visiting vessel. This information is passed along when you clear in at Suva.

The *sevu-sevu* ceremony is a meeting of the chief and the skipper. The yachtsman should greet the chief and explain the purpose of the visit. The chief replies with a formal speech of welcome. Then the islanders pass out the coconut cups of *kava*, which is a preparation of the dried root of a pepper plant. It is non-alcoholic, but somewhat tranquilizing. (It is customary for the guests to present a small bundle of these roots, available at any market, as a gift. Fijians and Tongans drink it all the time.) All the communicants then clap twice briskly, saying, "Bula, bula bula banaka", which translates as "Welcome! Thank you, thank you, very much." The cup goes around the circle, everyone making their thanks, and then they all imbibe.

The population is roughly half native Fijian, who own all the land, and half Indian, brought over a century ago as slaves. One hundred years ago, Fiji was a plantation colony of England and Australia. The planters did not wish to enslave the Fijians, so they imported Indians and other islanders, giving birth to the polyglot nation it now is.

Fiji today is multiracial. The Indians own and direct much of the commerce on the two big islands, and control much of the money wealth. The indigenous Fijians are settled along rivers and on the shores, and reap a good living from the land and sea. Despite some signs of discontent, race relations here are on the whole cooperative.

On the weather side of the Fiji Group is the Lau group. The Fijians in this Archipelago are the most traditional; their chiefs are proud, and wary of untoward influence they have witnessed elsewhere. The area is off limits to cruising boats unless they possess a special permit: research, religious or government-sponsored.

The Johnstone family, of yacht *Asteroid*, was granted this privilege, and Marguerite describes it here.

VANUATU

Sitting on the edge of the volcano and the New Hebrides Trench is Vanuatu, by all reports a unique and friendly island in Melanesia. It suffered some political birth pains wrenching free from the French-Anglo Condominion and various exploitative vigilantes. However, you don't see strife in the smiling faces of the islanders.

It is a populous nation of islands, a repository of multitudinous cultures and languages, and many traditional crafts. Strange and wonderful customs persist among some of these tribes. One constant in the culture is the importance of the pig; denoting wealth and authority, its curled tusk is currency, decoration and stuff of magic. Tropical flora rages through this large island group. Village commons are dominated by the great banyan tree.

Malakula Island is the home of the little Nambas, a primitive tribe that lives deep in the interior of Malakula. Missionaries have not penetrated this Stone Age sanctuary yet.

If you happen to pass this way in April, May or June, a ritual not to be missed is the Pentecost Land Dive. Tarzan fanciers will like this one. The islanders build a tower of branches, 80 to 100 feet, with platforms at various heights. The men attach a yam vine that is slightly shorter than the distance to the ground to their ankles, then dive. The vine breaks their fall. The provenance of the legend offers an ironic twist. The original successful diver was a woman, who had escaped to the tree tops from her husband, tied on a vine and dove. Her husband pursued her, and when she jumped he followed without the aid of a vine and died. All divers nowadays are male.

Rusting remnants of World War II artillery litter beaches here and on many islands in this part of the world. After the war, the U.S. army couldn't get the local planters to buy jeeps and other equipment used in the Guadalcanal campaign for two cents on the dollar, so the good soldiers drove them off the jetty. Anyone interested in diving on war wrecks can satiate themselves in this region.

ALISON LANGLEY

C.

D.

STEPHANIE BERKE

A. Yasawa Island Village
B. Market in Ovalou, Levuka Island
C. Church in Ovalou, Levuka Island
D. Anchorage in Yasawa Islands

TORRES STRAIT
Cape York
Thursday Is.
Port Darwin
Lizard
Cooktown
Cairns
Hinchinbrook Island
Townsville
Whitsunday Is.
AUSTRALIA
Shark Bay
Mooloolaba
Brisbane
Fremantle
Sydney
Adelaide
Kangaroo Island
TASMANIA
Port Davey
Hobart
NORTH ISLAND
Bay of Islands
Opua
Auckland
Wellington
Picton
COOK STRAIT
SOUTH ISLAND
Christchurch
Fjordland
Milford Sound
Stewart Is
NEW ZEALAND

DOWN UNDER

NEIL RABINOWITZ

tural export trade of New Zealand's finest. Sprawling across an isthmus between the Tasman Sea and the Pacific Ocean, Auckland is an excellent source for supply and repair. New Zealanders are descended from seafarers in all directions, which encourages them to be attuned to boats and hospitable to yachtsmen. Many foreign cruising boats layover here during the hurricane season, and use New Zealand as a base of operation for successive seasons of wandering in the western Pacific. There are beautiful beaches, good restaurants with outdoor dining, and all the cultural attractions one could desire.

The Hauraki Gulf east of Auckland is bordered by the Coromandel Peninsula. This peninsula has spectacular topography formed by recent glaciers with a full spectrum of temperate landscapes. There are rugged sheer cliffs, forests, and rolling pasture land undulating down to the sea. Inland are A.

NEW ZEALAND TOURIST OFFICE

hotsprings and geysers.

A sailor writes:

Sailing down the Coromandel Peninsula you pass White Island, Tongariro's host... voluminous clouds of steam, and the stench of real fire and brimstone coming from its crater; the approach and passage, the awesome sight is with you for quite a while.

Mercury Bay is an inlet dotted with small islands on the east coast of the Coromandel Peninsula which points north, like a finger, between the Bay of Plenty and the Hauraki Gulf in the North Island of New Zealand.

It was at Mercury Bay that seafarer Captain James Cook hoisted the English flag on November 15, 1769, to formally take possession of the land for his King, George III.

Captain Cook, on his voyage of discovery in the South Pacific, anchored the *Endeavour* in the bay to set up a shore station on Cook's Beach (as it is now called) in order to observe the transit of the planet Mercury. Before departing, he named the bay Mercury in memory of the occasion.

The main settlement in the bay today is Whitianga (permanent population 2000) which overlooks the placid estuary where boats lie at anchor. The Mercury Bay area did a roaring trade in the early days with the felling of the native *kauri* tree which is currently still a sought-after timber. The *kauri* tree compares in majesty with the Californian redwood. The local wharf, used to get the timber out to ships waiting to transport it to civilization, was built with stones from an old Maori fort on the headland nearby.

The area is a significant one to the native Maori people of New Zealand. Kupe, their legendary explorer, is said to have crossed the narrow entrance to the harbor on his famed voyage through New Zealand one thousand years ago. The name *Whitianga-a-Kupe*, to give the settlement its full Maori title, translates "the crossing of Kupe."

Gold drew the more mercenary European settler to the area during the last century when diggers from Californian and Australian fields rushed in for hectic, short-lived prosperity.

A. Russell, Bay of Islands
B. Secluded anchorage, Bay of Islands
C. Bay of Plenty

ALISON LANGLEY

B.

C.

NEW ZEALAND TOURIST OFFICE

NEW ZEALAND TOURIST OFFICE

A.

B.

NEW ZEALAND TOURIST OFFICE

Big-game fishing is another attraction at Mercury Bay. The season runs December 26 through April, with February and March providing the best fishing: tuna, black and striped marlin, mako and thresher sharks, and kingfish abound.

Initiated by New Zealand's controversial America's Cup challenge in San Diego in 1988, the Coromandel Peninsula is grabbing the attention of many people around the world.

New Zealand's capital city of Wellington possesses an enchanting if rather inaccessible harbor. It is extremely well protected and charming: resembling San Francisco in hills, gardens, arts and gracious architecture. The terrifically boisterous waters that meet here at the southern tip of the North Island effectively prohibit most cruising boats from getting there. In the Cook Straits, the Swan 65, *Show Me*, encountered the worst weather the crew had seen in three years since leaving California. For twelve hours they battled wind rising from 10 to 60 knots in a matter of minutes, williwaw gusts from the mountains, and monstrous seas from all quarters.

SOUTH ISLAND

Across the Cook Straits, in incredibly beautiful Marlborough Sounds is the sweet little harbor of Picton, the gateway to the South Island. A rare treat for the cruising sailor is the company of penguins that live here. New Zealand has 250 species of birds, among them the Kiwi, of course, and several other species of flightless fowl.

The entire South Island is dramatic and merits some thorough inland investigation. Way down on the south end is majestic Fjordland. Milford Sound is replete with fjords and the waters are extremely steep to. The best way to sail there is probably on a cruise ship. Inland there are fabulous rivers, cascades and glaciers; turquoise-blue mountain lakes repose under snow-capped peaks. Trout streams weave through lush green pastures awash with lupine, in every color imaginable. In this rugged country, trekkers, skiiers, fishermen and rafters can really explore, by getting heli-lifted to the remote destination of their dreams.

A. Aerial of Picton Harbor
B. Wellington, North Island
C. Marlborough Sound
D. Mitre Peak, Milford Sound Park

NEIL RABINOWITZ

C.

D.

NEIL RABINOWITZ

PATRICIA DENT

A.

I particularly like Sydney Harbor, because I usually go there to cover the Sydney - Hobart Yacht Race which starts the day after Christmas. The memory of spending the New Year cooled by the balmy breezes of the Southern Hemisphere makes me lose all objectivity. What's special about Sydney Harbor is the size of the sailable surface and the changing backdrop views you have from one "fjord" to another.

You could spend over a week cruising in Sydney Harbor, discover a new landscape every day and daily drink a different lager in a different yacht club.

Sailing in the harbor you would have to avoid the water-taxis, the hydrofoil ferries, the crews of the 18-footers hiking out on their trapezes or standing on foldout ladders like circus artists, and of course you would have to watch out for all different types of yachts coming and going from one of the many yacht clubs.

If you want to watch the harbor activities from the shore, because you are only here on a stopover, you can sit on a bench in a park, have lunch at the Opera House, look down from the cliffs of Sydney's North Head or even take a dip off one of the nude beaches. Yes, there are three of them in the harbor! If you spend more than three days "down under" the friendly Australians almost certainly make sure you see the harbor from the waterlevel!

And if you sail into the harbor at dark and are suddenly frightened by the roar of an African lion, it doesn't mean you made a navigational error and are landing on the wrong continent. You just strayed a bit to close to the northern shore where one of the most beautiful zoos in the world overlooks the harbor.

Daniel

Daniel Forster
Swiss Marine Photographer

A. Sydney Harbor
B. S/Y Show Me anchored at White Rock

AUSTRALIA

Sydney, Australia is in Port Jackson, a perfect natural harbor that was identified and named by explorer James Cook in 1770. It was originally the forced haven of thousands of British convicts and paupers, and has grown to be the most prominent and culturally active city in Australia.

As Port Jackson has many prongs and inlets, the city of Sydney has a long coastline. On one of these peninsulas are the buildings of the Government Domain and a park crowned by the signature landmark of the Sydney Opera House.

Australia is unique among the continents of the world. Isolated by its remoteness, and inhabited by a non-seafaring aboriginal people, the evolution of plant and animal life developed quite independent of the rest of the world. It is also very arid in the interior, so when settlement from the Europeans eventually came, it was restricted to the coasts. Much of the west coast is climatically harsh, so it is the eastern coast of Australia that is abundantly populated.

The East Coast from Sydney south is a beautiful cruising ground undiscovered by most cruising sailors, except for those bound for Tasmania. Australia is a nation of sailors, so the bays and marinas of this entire coast are filled with Aussie craft.

ALISON LANGLEY

B.

COURTESY OF MIRAGE RESORTS

A.

B.

NEIL RABINOWITZ

The Great Barrier Reef shelters a concentration of stunning anchorages. The inside passage is deep and well-charted, but access through the reef is always limited by draft, and especially tricky at the northern end. Many cruising sailors approach the Great Barrier Reef by way of Mooloolaba, on the old Morechtydore River just north of Brisbane. This coast is a lee shore, and Mooloolaba offers a good secure haven from which to strike out briefly and then tuck in behind the reef. It breaks up a stretch of some of the world's best surfing beach. That may be an enchantment to some sailors, but it also gives an indication of navigational difficulties. The entry into the harbor is prone to sand bars. Mooloolaba is a port of entry, a nice town, and a good general supply port.

The Whitsunday Island group is beautiful, and a regular stop on the cruising sailor's pilgrimage. The steep walled fjord of Nara Inlet on Hook Island is a popular refuge. Testimonial to this fact is in an anchorage at the head of the inlet where the painted names of visiting boats artfully decorate a sloping incline of black lava rock.

Dunk Island and many of the other islands here are largely national park. Dunk Island was discovered and chronicled in the early part of the century by E.J. Banfield; Australia's equivalent of

C.

North of Townsville, on the windward side of Hinchinbrook Island, lies Zoe Bay. It is a wide bay with a creek to the north and a creek to the south. The southern creek is shallow. I anchored my catamaran with orchids literally dripping onto my deck, and parrots squawking in the jungle.

The view is dramatic, similar to Moorea, with high pointed peaks. A long beach, lined with coconuts, joins the two creeks.

There are no villages, no roads, no tourists. On the south creek, just past a small sign erected by the Wildlife Department warning of crocodiles, is a path winding through tropical rain forest to a year round waterfall. The deep, cool pool below it is a great watering spot, since the dinghy may be taken up to where the water becomes fresh. A true Australian Paradise.

Peter Carr

Peter Carr
Australian Artist/Traveler

Thoreau. He fled the hustle of Townsville to absorb and contemplate the sanctity and solitude of nature; "to gaze dreamily at the filigree of reef across the endless blue; and to seek under the forest canopy for butterflies and birds of color." These islands are inhabited by a hundred species of birds: the sunbird, the osprey, sea eagles, cockatoos, pheasants, jungle fowl, parrots, and many many more. There are a few resorts, also Banfield's farm, restaurant and gardens. The Australian forestry service seems to have achieved a good balance in this area providing services for a limited number of people to explore an exotic wilderness close at hand.

There are countless splendid anchorages in the shelter of the Great Barrier Reef. Zoe Bay on the huge National Park of Hinchinbrook Island is one of the most spectacular. Here again the quintessential palm-fringed beaches give way to a sloping rainforest, replete with waterfalls and vines, and great multitudes of tropical birds.

Cooktown is a ghost town left over from the Palmer River Gold Rush. Farther north on the Great Barrier Reef is Lizard Island, a world-reknowned outpost for game fishing.

A. Mirage III cruising by Port Douglas
B. Anchorage in the Whitsundays
C. Lizard Island

ALISON LANGLEY

A.

ALISON LANGLEY

B.

WEST AUSTRALIA

The West Coast of Australia is wild and not particularly enticing as a cruising ground. Shark Bay is one enclosure which does offer a variety of good anchorages, in addition to lots of fish including its namesake. The water here is quite cold and inhabited by a quantity of sharks, huge manta rays, and sea snakes.

Flanked by tall sand cliffs, dunes, and desert shrub, the land has a savage beauty. The turquoise waters are dazzling. Cruising sailor, Alison Langley, writes of rolling and strolling on the glorious dunes, warming up after a quick swim. She and her fellow crew members even saw a dingo canter by.

In contrast to the forbidding prospect of swimming in much of this area, nearby is Monkey Mia Bay. This place has an opposite phenomenon that fulfills the dreams of nature lovers: a dolphin playground where the happy denizens welcome the visit of gamboling playmates. Have you ever wanted to jump in and swim with those friendly dolphins? They have kept sailors company on many a watch, and we think we feel some rapport and response. Well, here is a bay where, for some reason the dolphins will humor you, let you get a good look, and even let you pet them.

Alison Langley described her experience in their midst:

...The exhilaration of being in the midst of half a dozen happy dolphins! We brought along two buckets of fish and headed ashore. Actually I hopped out of the boat before we got there because the dolphins were right alongside— I couldn't wait to touch them! We spent the morning swimming, patting and playing with the dolphins. They really are such happy creatures. When you stroked their sides they'd click contentedly, like a cat would purr...

The commercial port of Fremantle gained the world's attention and drew a huge volume of yachts when the America's Cup Races were held there in 1987. It was the first time the Cup left American soil and sailors from all over

C.

D.

the world convened here to witness the much-publicized challenge.

Natural wonders in some of the most bizarre animal forms are often associated with Australia. Large parts of Kangaroo Island, off South Australia, are conservation preserves of those unique Aussie creatures. This island has several good anchorages. It has a concentrated version of the Australian frontier history, replete with prisoners, pirates and struggling immigrants.

American River at Pelican Lagoon is a wondrous anchorage, an inland sea among emerald-clothed ridges. Here, for instance, you could leave the boat and take a camel trek of three to five days into the bush, and see the kangaroos and other wildlife against a landscape of immense rock cliffs.

Sailing the southern waters between Australia and Melbourne, an abundance of sea life can be observed. Yachtsmen report seeing whales, sea lions, and dolphins from horizon to horizon. Australian sea lions and New Zealand fur seals, native to this coast, were spared the decimations of sealing last century. For wind-powered vessels, the coast is rocky and forbidding; thus the establishment of many sealing stations was prevented.

A. S/V Eye of the Wind in Shark Bay
B. Cape York, Queensland
C. Sand dune, Peron Peninsula
D. Friendly porpoise of Monkey Mia

ALISON LANGLEY

A.

ALISON LANGLEY

STEPHANIE BERKE

A.

B.

STEPHANIE BERKE

eat with their hands from a great mountain of food. Often they bring some of the villagers aboard to return the hospitality. Much good rapport has been engendered in these gatherings.

The Trobriand Islands are a beautiful archipelago where a lot of the finest, most elaborate ebony carvings come from. Intricate *story boards*, which often deal with the creation myths, tell how the people arrived originally in a spiritual canoe, and lived in a cave. The *story boards* also depict their fertility rites and their relationship to nature. This interesting craft is also typical to Yap and Pelau.

Port Moresby, New Guinea was made famous by General MacArthur's World War II exploits here. The devastation of this occupation still litters the jungle and coast, as well as the underwater world.

Nearly anytime you venture inland and up in this part of the world, you let yourself in for an incredible cultural adventure. One traveler reports a six-hour hike inland to a highland village, without ever seeing cars, bikes or electricity. She did witness some fantastically primitive people. The *Mud People* pictured here are an example. Authentic trading ceremonies all over Indonesia and Polynesia are thrilling when you are fortunate enough to encounter them.

The general neighborhood around Papua New Guinea is a garden of island delights. Goodenough Island rises sharply out of a turquoise sea to 2600 feet. Anchorage in its shadow is further embellished by the grand green sentinels of the peaks of Papua. The Duke of York island group is spectacular, noted for its ancient trees.

Volcanic activity under this region provides boiling undersea hot springs which make for an interesting anchorage. Esa'Ala in the d'Entrecasteaux group is one such delightful anchorage. Lovely, laughing, flower-festooned women are a common attraction of this glorious island region. The women, the children and the fascinating diversity of legends and ceremonies make sailing to this part of the world an unforgettable experience.

In Rabaul, on the island of New Britain, Papua New Guinea, the natives

STEPHANIE BERKE

C.

D.

QUEENSLAND TOURIST & TRAVEL

traditionally paint themselves in brilliant colors or cake themselves with mud. This spectacular harbor is actually located within the crater of a dormant volcano. The bay is surrounded by jungle covered cones (the harbor is evacuated periodically when an eruption appears imminent). Rabaul was a major Japanese port and airfield during World War II. There are hundreds of wrecks to dive on, and military complexes to see in the surrounding jungle.

Some sailing friends had a mission there recently, at 135 feet down. One of the crew, years ago, had taken a femur bone out of a wreck, and had since been told it was bad luck. So on this trip he dove to repair the kharma and replace the bone of the departed sailor.

A. Mud men of Papua New Guinea
B. Spirit house, New Guinea
C. S/Y Shirley B. at D'Entrecasteaux Archipelago
D. Underwater adventures

ALISON LANGLEY

A.

B.

ALISON LANGLEY

PALAU

The island nation which is now called Palau sits atop the Pacific *Ring of Fire*, a ring of submerged volcanos along the Belau trench, 27,000 feet deep, where tectonic plates meet. The past century has brought cataclysmic change of a cultural variety. Nineteenth century contacts with passing ships introduced modern ideas and disease to this native culture. The archipelago was used as military headquarters in both world wars, further infecting the age-old culture in most of the island group.

Lying 80 miles from the larger islands in this group, the people of the southwest islands of this archipelago are the most primitive. The islands are extremely underpopulated and empty now, but the legends tell of a canoe-borne fleet which left Yap because of overpopulation there, and came to settle here. Eventually wanderers moved to the more provident islands in the north.

The people of Palau are simple, yet their traditions are complex. The succession of chiefs, hereditary and chosen, has survived many years of foreign rule. The ceremonial exchange of gifts, time, money and services on special occasions in their lives is still very important. Diving on the Helen Reef is spectacular.

NICOLA DENT

C. D.

BARRY BAILEY

A. Rabaul Harbor, New Guinea
B. B-26 bomber, Rabaul
C. Helen Reef, Palau
D. Rock Islands, Helen Reef

JAPAN

The ancient history of Japan is extensively maritime, being a nation of islands enclosing an inland sea. The large inter-Asian trade began to decline in the 13th century when the Emperor was challenged by the military *shogun*. Then, for 200 insular years while Europe was expanding into and exploiting Asia, the *shoguns* refused all trade and foreign influence with any country but China. After repeated attempts, the American, Commodore Perry, finally succeeded in 1853 in gaining a foothold there for trade and fortifications. Dissatisfied with the military rule, Emperor Meiji threw over the *shogun*, and decided to cooperate with Perry and open Japan to the modern world. Here began an intensive and elaborately engineered metamorphosis, by which Japan took a one-hundred-year leap from a medieval economy into an enormous industrial empire.

On a coast which is blessed with many natural harbors, several ports were developed in the course of this meteoric rise. These ports were thoroughly planned and executed from the start, unencumbered by the baggage of old technology. Like everything Japanese, shipping and cargo is efficiently carried out.

The original delta port of Osaka traditionally served the spiritual center of Kyoto, and a similar relationship occurred between Yokohama and the financial center of Tokyo. When deep draught vessels entered the scene, the channels were dredged, and artificial islands were created for industry, a common feature today in Japan.

Lack of resources drove the Japanese to imperialism to fuel their industry, but World War II brought their territorial expansion to an abrupt halt. Since that time, Japanese economic expansion has continued to grow through international cooperation and management of human resources.

With over a hundred ports in its indented coastline, Japan handles about one third of the world's shipping.

A society so insulated and so rigorously controlled by spirituality and the military, did not develop much in

ALISON LANGLEY

A.

JAPAN NAT'L TOURIST OFFICE

B.

C.

JAPAN NAT'L TOURIST OFFICE

ALISON LANGLEY

D.

E.

ALISON LANGLEY

A. S/Y Show Me anchored near Aburatsubo
B. Kumomi fishing port with Mt. Fuji in background
C. Kumomi coast
D. Prayer flags and cherry blossoms
E. Rowing in the Izu Hanto Peninsula

the way of leisure watersports until its mighty leap into prosperity. Marinas and yacht harbors are now part of the planned development on these islands of land reclamation.

Sailing is considered very expensive and esoteric in Japan, hardly the average man's pastime. But more than the cost of yachting, the biggest anomaly to the Japanese mentality is taking off from the work-a-day world to go cruising. The lifestyle of the cruising sailor is by and large out of their ken. Perhaps this is changing.

Aburatsubo, near Kamakura in the gulf of Yokohama, is the oldest yacht harbor in Japan. This was the first landfall of *Show Me*, a Swan 65, which made a fairly extensive tour in Japanese waters. Captain Herb Kiendl reported that the logistics of mooring and clearing are still rather cumbersome, but he was impressed with the majestic views surrounding every harbor. It was April, and the cherry blossoms were in bloom; the crew embarked on several reconnaissance missions by bicycle through quaint fishing villages on this peninsula. Aburatsubo was a good base for one and two day excursions to the lakes and mountains inland, like Hakone Machi.

The fishing port of Shimoda on the Izu hanto peninsula has importance in Japanese-American relations. After Perry with his *black ships* forced the opening of trade with the west, the first American diplomat, Townsend Harris, lived in Shimoda with his Japanese consort. The novel *Shogun* portrayed this saga.

The huge natural harbor of Osaka in spite of being industrial, is still beautiful. The yacht club in Osaka is landscaped in formal gardens and equipped with a health club, running courses and bike trail. As a result of dredging, the city of Osaka is intertwined with canals. This is an excellent base for exploring Kyoto and Nara, and temples of incomparable beauty. Kobe, in Osaka Bay, is the location of several yacht-building yards.

Herb Kiendl said that the most enchanting harbor he visited in Japan was on a private island near Tamano in the Inland Sea, where the crew met a Japanese man in his launch. The crew was invited to wine and dine lavishly and share boating stories in a land where visiting sailors are still a novelty. The Japanese were extremely hospitable.

Fukuoka is a traditional Japanese harbor on the Asian side of Kyushu. To reach there you leave the relative tranquility of the Inland Sea and brave the tidal turbulence of these waters as they ebb and flow to the Sea of Japan. The Straits of Shimonoseki, between Honshu and Kyushu, have currents up to 12 knots; the traffic is so busy that they have tugs standing by to pull, and digital readout on the current, congestion and conditions in the straits.

HONG KONG

The streets and waters of Hong Kong exemplify the zenith of busy exchange that a true port becomes. In this respect it is interesting to look at Canton, the port that Hong Kong was destined to replace.

For centuries, the port of Canton was a city of merchants, with a long enduring history of open doors to the world. It was the only Chinese port allowed to trade with the outside world. Sampans and junks, cargos and lighters, ferries and tugs have long plied the Pearl River from Hong Kong, hailing from ports afar, to take part in the Cantonese market. A large bulk of this commerce was originally a significant trade in opium.

These mercantile roots go way back. Roman traders are said to have journeyed to Canton 1000 years before Marco Polo reached China. Those fabled merchant quests for silk, tea and spices led to the walled city of Canton. It was not only an important foreign trade center for Chinese goods. In the 18th century the mercantile atmosphere attracted foreign merchants with their goods for mutual trade. They set up their businesses, "hongs", along the Pearl also.

During the Opium Wars in the 1840s, a British plenipotentiary annexed Hong Kong to assuage British losses in Canton, and conserve an international entrepôt for commerce and carenage. The Cultural Revolution further constrained Canton's access to the trade, and so Hong Kong, ("fragrant harbor"), an amazing cultural hybrid, was created, populated and built upon to take its place.

The fortunes of Hong Kong also have waxed and waned with the political vicissitudes of Southeast Asia. Hong Kong harnessed the hordes of refugees from communist China into a vast work force, a giant sweatshop for textiles. Quality of production eventually improved, along with harbor facilities. Today, it is a giant, fascinating marketplace; and some reassuring shade of western culture in Asia allows us, the *gaijin*, a closer glimpse of Chinese people and culture.

ALISON LANGLEY

A.

B.

ALISON LANGLEY

Aberdeen is the old harbor that is replete with junks and sampans, the remains of the former throngs of refugee boat dwellers. The Yacht Harbor is around on the Kowloon side. The Peak which rises so unexpectedly behind the harbor can be reached by funicular. It's cool up there, and the view is superb.

Canton revived too; the tradition of buying, selling, and personal enterprise is back, flourishing along the drifting panorama of the river Pearl. Its streets are still thronged with independent vendors, selling their little stock of edible or useful trade. Everyone is a merchant. In the meantime, Hong Kong has far exceeded the bulk of trade and is a hive of manufacturing.

ALISON LANGLEY

C. D.

ALISON LANGLEY

THE PHILIPPINES

Fertile land, enormous miles of coastline and munificent seas have blessed the inhabitants of this great archipelago since time immemorial. Filipino fortunes have only recently come into world view with the outrages of the Marcos family and ensuing rule of Corazon Aquino. These political disturbances seem to be less of a hindrance to the sailing tourist than the age-old menace of pirates in the Sulu Sea to the south.

The Filipino resisted little when the Spanish arrived with the sword and the cross. A good-natured, flexible group, they absorbed the fiesta along with Catholicism, and remained complacent when the Americans took over after the Spanish-American War. Four hundred years of Latin dominion, followed by seventy of American, has created a Melanesian-Malay-Latin-Gringo hybrid which is totally unique in the world.

Puerto Galero, Mindoro just opposite Betangas, the industrial port on Luzon, is a beautiful protected harbor. The lovely Filipinos carry on their fishing, growing, crafts and daily life against a quintessential tropical backdrop of swaying palms and mountain glory. Spanish galleons used to moor here, so for divers there is another older dimension to explore, and the possibility of finding Spanish wrecks and pieces of eight. Cebu, in the Phillipines, is becoming a flourishing center for yacht construction.

A. Marina Cove & Hebe Haven, Hong Kong Harbor
B. Drying bêche de mer
C. Sailing in Hong Kong Harbor
D. Fishing in" Fragrant Harbor"

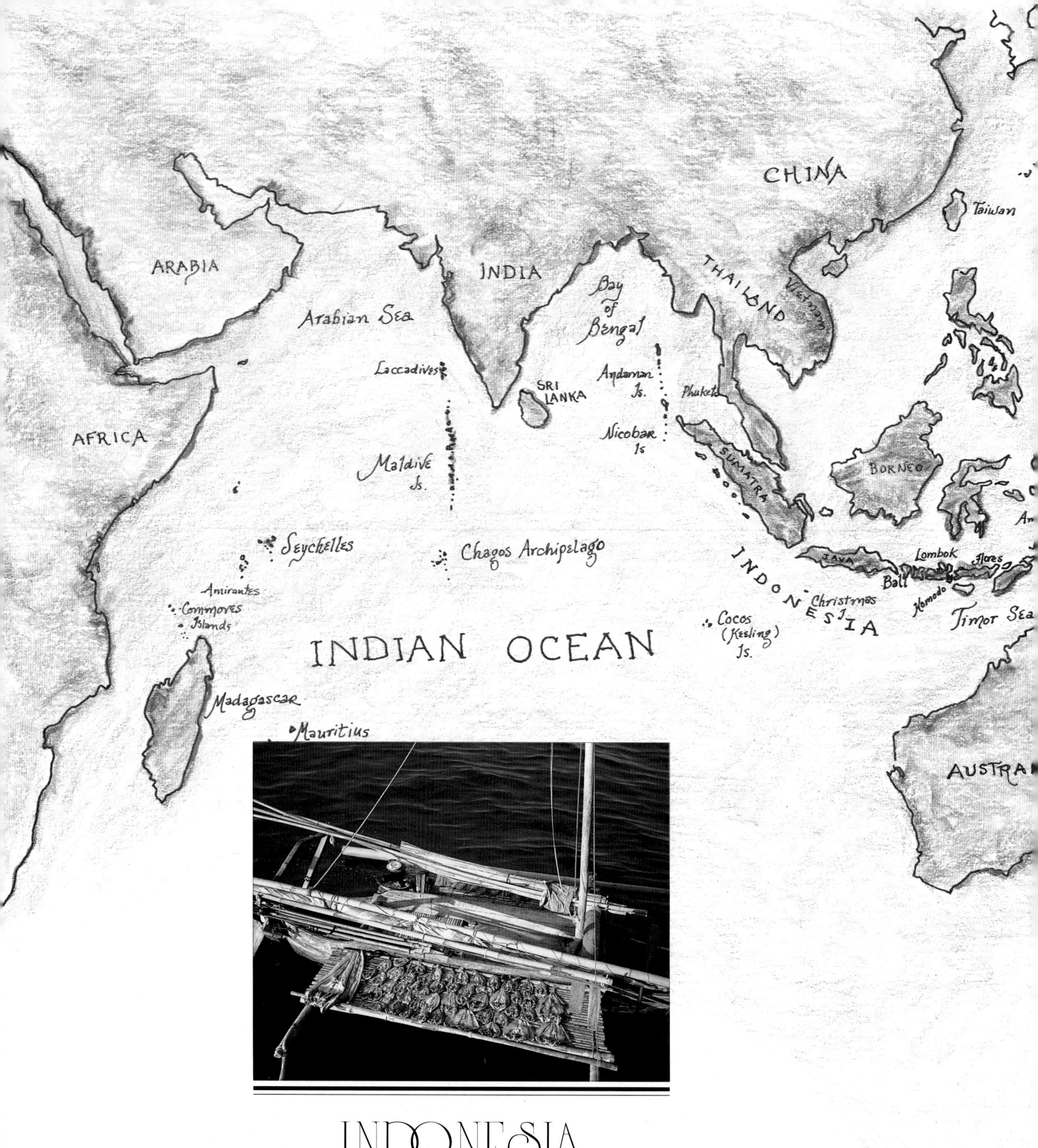

INDONESIA & THE INDIAN OCEAN

NICOLA DENT

INDONESIA

Indonesia, a string of pearls between India and Australia, is a land of prodigious wealth and cultural diversity. The land is endowed with rich volcanic soil, traditional equatorial crops, and its main source of wealth: minerals. The population is an incredible mélange of natives and transplants.

The only species that has not really taken root there is "the tourist". The various governments have not quite tackled the issue of cruising permits, so the uncertainty here may be one deterrent to yachtsmen. Because of the extreme volcanic nature of the place, anchorages are often sheer drop-offs and require a stern line tied to a tree. However, we have heard nothing but favorable reports from those who have managed to sail here.

The aroma of clove and cinnamon wafted across Eurasia from the Spice Islands for many centuries along the overland caravan route. The Chinese had also visited Indonesia for sandalwood and beeswax. However, it wasn't until Vasco da Gama from Portugal linked his quest for riches and nautical discovery with the 15th Century Crusades against the Muslim Empire that European trade and conquest of the Indies began in earnest.

Preceding page Thai fisherwomen

A. A sleepy morning in Banda
B. Looking down on Banda from the volcano
C. A Kora Kora war canoe visiting S/V Lene Marie

Cruising in Indonesia has been limited in the past few decades. Generally, a permit to enter Indonesian waters has to be applied for in Jakarta well in advance. It is possible to apply for a permit to stay for more than two months: however, there is a catch in this, because you can only get a normal visa for two months. If you want to stay longer, you will have to fly out (Singapore or Australia) and return, or come to a special "arrangement" with the authorities.

An increasingly popular method used over the past few years to get around this permit problem is to enter an annual race for cruising yachts from Darwin or another Australian port to Bali. Entry into one of these races means that you have a reasonable chance of getting a cruising permit. After the race, the return trip to Australia can be sailed at a more leisurely pace.

Benoa is a natural harbour and about the only port in Bali into which it is possible to gain easy access. The entrance is quite narrow, and not so easy to negotiate, it looks almost as if you will end up amongst the breakers on Sanur beach that runs northward from the harbour entrance. Stick to the markers and you will be okay, providing the wind is not from the east or northeast.

Bali is a beautiful place to visit: the people are friendly, they have an amazing culture, and the countryside is beautiful. Rent a bike or a "bemo" for a day or two and take off to the rice paddies.

Patricia Dent

Patricia Dent
Sailor/ Journalist

NICOLA DENT

A.

THE MOLUCCAS

Once the Portuguese gained a foothold in the Moluccas (or Malukas), fleets and adventurers of various other nationalities joined the migration; notably the Dutch. The Banda Islands were once the nutmeg capital of the world, as well as a source for textiles and other tropical items coveted in Europe. The Dutch planters built their forts and villas around this lovely tropical chain. Today the force of that trade has slackened and the nutmeg distinction has gone to the island of Grenada, in the Caribbean. The history, edifices, and artifacts of the era of European dominion remain, enhancing the natural beauty. The local people are extremely friendly and curious.

The traditional war canoes, the *kora koras*, were used to defend the islands against intruders. Nowadays they bring them out to greet visiting dignitaries and often festoon them for village celebrations.

NICOLA DENT

B.

C.

JOHN DONOVAN

JOHN DONOVAN

A.

B.

KELVIN JONES

A. S/V Lene Marie anchored in Komodo
B. Komodo dragon
C. Port of Saumlaki on Tanimbar
D. Lombok, Indonesia

KOMODO

Nearby to the west is the island of Komodo, home of the fabled Komodo dragons, which are unique to this island. They grow as long as 10 feet and feed on deer, boar and goats in the wild. This species of monitor lizard appears to be deaf and immobile, and requires solar heat to get going. Occasionally they do sprint,and unlike most lizards,they can swim. You can visit the monsters in quasi-captivity, under the auspices of the nature rangers. In lieu of an admission fee, it is recommended that visitors purchase a goat to feed the lizards. We don't advertise visiting the small fishing harbor here. The seas around Komodo are roiling with whirlpools and turbulence, accentuating the various myths and theories about the supernatural provenance of these creatures. It is best to come over on the ferry from Bajo.

Indonesian ethnic diversity is broadly illustrated on Flores and the islands nearby. The language and physical stature of the natives varies greatly from Melanesia to Malay. The Portuguese and Dutch left their influence on many of the more urban communities. Anyone who takes the time will discover a cornucopia of ethnological wonders.

KELVIN JONES

C.

STEPHANIE BERKE

D.

Komodo was once a penal colony with a terrible reputation and little chance for escape, since terrific rip currents and whirlpools circle the island and give even moderately large boats a shake up on their approach. It is now a national park; visitors can arrange for a government guide to take them in search of the "dragons". A goat is taken as bait, slaughtered and suspended over a dry ravine where the lizards are known to frequent. Sometimes as many as 20 lizards appear, but on this occasion, only five or six show up. They are not particularly hungry either since they have had visitors on the four previous days. This is just as well, for visitors would not be allowed out of the stockade above, and down into the ravine if the beasts were hungry and more active. They have been known to rear up on their hind legs and run at surprising speed. Last year they even managed to eat a lone photographer who was foolish enough to camp overnight unprotected.

Kelvin Jones
Photographer

BALI

The harbor at Benoa in Bali is nothing to write home about, but Bali is. Balinese culture regards the sea as the province of demons; hence, the natives have never become fishermen or seafarers. They eat fish, but their orientation is toward the land. Dramatic mountainous terrain does not deter the resourceful Balinese from agricultural pursuits: the terraced rice paddies are functional and beautiful. Bali is included here because it provides entry to one of the most unforgettable cultural experiences that cruising the world has to offer.

Balinese society respects privacy and the individual, as is evident in the home and village structure. However, they are also intensely communal in social, agricultural, creative and religious pursuits. Their spirituality is a strong presence in everyday life, yet not overbearing. The people seem to have imported the faith, art and music of Hinduism, and combined it with the existing Balinese beliefs in animism. They hold that the good spirits inhabit the mountains, the demons' domain is under the sea, and various mischiefs haunt the woods and desolate beaches. Their daily lives are filled with rituals and offerings, dances and prayers to contain the good and lofty graces. The composite of this culture is immensely intricate, but surprisingly visible to the respectful, inquisitive traveler.

The crafts, carvings, and textile arts were always regarded as a byproduct of worship, never as an achievement or individual skill. The onslaught of tourism has, of course, created a market for a profusion of crafts, yet the most quotidian crafts that represent their spirituality — all the small trinkets, trays, offerings, palm braids and harmonious arrangements of food — are done with love and beauty.

PATRICIA DENT

A.

B.

PATRICIA DENT

KELVIN JONES

C. D. E.

PATRICIA DENT

STEPHANIE BERKE

A. Bow of Balinese outrigger
B. Balinese fisherman
C. Balinese musicians
D. Prahu under full sail
E. Terraced rice paddies

TOURISM AUTHORITY OF THAILAND

A.

KELVIN JONES

B.

C.

BILL ROBINSON

PHUKET

The island of Phuket is a fast-growing tourist resort that celebrates all the natural attributes of a tropical paradise. Imagine white sand, azure seas, swaying palms– all in the shadow of majestic high jungles–served up with cool drinks, privacy, and a smile. Meandering masseurs offer beachside therapy to complete the indulgence. To a cruising sailor, Phuket also presents a safe harbor from which to launch an overland tour of the real Thailand.

The fishing village of Rawai, on the southern tip, is a land base of the sea gypsies, the *chao lay*, who used to live exclusively at sea.

There are a great many small, enticing islands in the Andaman Sea near Phuket. The steep limestone cliffs of these islands are pierced with caves. One was used in a James Bond film; hence, it is now known as James Bond Island. A traveling journalist, Kelvin Jones, who supplied these photos, says that people collect swallows' nests from the many caves on these islands for birds nest soup. Perhaps a Thai local was pulling his leg. At any rate, Jones claims that the ropes and poles are the equipment of the nest gatherers. Phi Phi Island, (pronounced Pi Pi) is one of these romantic islands.

Thai cuisine is most worthy of mention. The Thai people enhance the natural fresh essence of their seafood, fruit, meat and vegetables with coconut milk and a legion of hot chilis, cilantro, lime and other distinctive spices. Phuket enjoys a wealth of delicious seafood. The market is wonderful for aromas and also for a colorful display of fabrics for sarongs.

A. Local boat ferrying tourists
B. Spice and vegetable market
C. The ultimate tropical island of Phi Phi
D. "James Bond Island"

KELVIN JONES

D.

THE MALDIVES

The Andaman and Nicobar Islands are somewhat restricted to cruising boats, although many stop there to break up the trip. The Maldives are the customary and preferred cruising group in the Arabian Sea.

The Maldives chain extends for 1000 miles north and south to the west of Sri Lanka, an aggregation of beautiful beaches and largely uninhabited coral atolls. It has never been colonized, per se, but was a British protectorate from 1887 to 1965; hence, English is spoken in the port town of Male. Tourism is gradually changing this quiet fishing economy, but most of the commotion occurs only in the main port.

Cocos (Keeling) atoll is one of the best anchorages in the world. It has a small indigenous Malay population.

PATRICIA DENT

A.

B.

STEPHANIE BERKE

PATRICIA DENT

C.

D.

STEPHANIE BERKE

STEPHANIE BERKE

E.

A. Local boats, South Andaman
B. Toddu Atoll, Maldives
C. Market, South Andaman
D. Male, Maldives
E. Maldivian girl

STEPHANIE BERKE

A.

B.

STEPHANIE BERKE

CHAGOS

About 1000 miles east of the Seychelles is the Chagos Archipelago, scattered across several hundred miles of ocean. This is an idyllic group, uninhabited, and filled with secure anchorages. The local populace was moved to the Mauritius' when the United States leased the archipelago as a military base. Consequently, buildings, plantations, and remnants of settlements are scattered along the atolls. The military headquarters are on the island of Diego Garcia, and are rigorously off-limits. Many lovely and safe anchorages can be found, however, in the Salomon Islands or Peros Banhos. Diving is excellent.

A. Cocoa Island, Maldives
B. Fairy terns
C. Chagos Atoll
D. Amirante Isles, Seychelles

BARRY BAILEY

C.

D.

JOHN DONOVAN

SEYCHELLES

The granite peaks of a submerged continent break out of the Indian Ocean as the Seychelle Islands. No volcanic eruption or coral growth created it. It is just the top of a sunken world. Totally uninhabited until 200 years ago, the Seychelles were an occasional roost for merchant traders and pirates. The French planters arrived in 1750 and imported slaves from Africa and several other nations.

One hundred years later, with slavery abolished, intermarriage had produced a very handsome race of Creole culture. British, Indian, French, Chinese, African and Arabic peoples blend their colors, creating a fine featured, coffee-colored people. Their overall temperment is quite pleasing. Their language is Creole and so is their cuisine—primarily spicy fish and vegetable dishes.

Mahe is the main town. All the other islands were individual plantations. On Praslin Island, in a nature preserve called the Vallee de Mai, luxuriant plants grow in a garden of Eden. Here grows the sensual, bilobed *coco de mer*, whose coconut resembles the anatomy of a voluptuous woman. They say its nectar is an aphrodisiac. The Seychelles are also home to several other rare species of flora and fauna.

NICOLA DENT

A. B.

NICOLA DENT

PATRICIA DENT

C.

D.

A few years ago I was marooned in the Maldives and allowed myself to get shanghaied to the Seychelles.

It was a miserable trip. We were either slogging to windward, or becalmed with sails flopping on a rolly sea. With tempers flaring, and the cupboards looking paltry, we were happy to hit the Seychelles.

The crew headed for a day at the beach. A swim felt great after the passage, but no sooner had we brought out our picnic... and the bullets started flying. A gentleman with a wide brimmed hat, next to us on the beach, murmured something about another "coup"... and kept on reading. I guess the politics of the Seychelles are as fluky as the winds of the Indian Ocean...

Lucy Morales

Lucy Morales
Argentinian tap dancer

KELVIN JONES

A. Beachcomber in the Seychelles
B. Victoria Harbor
C. Secluded beach, Seychelles
D. Young Indonesian sailors

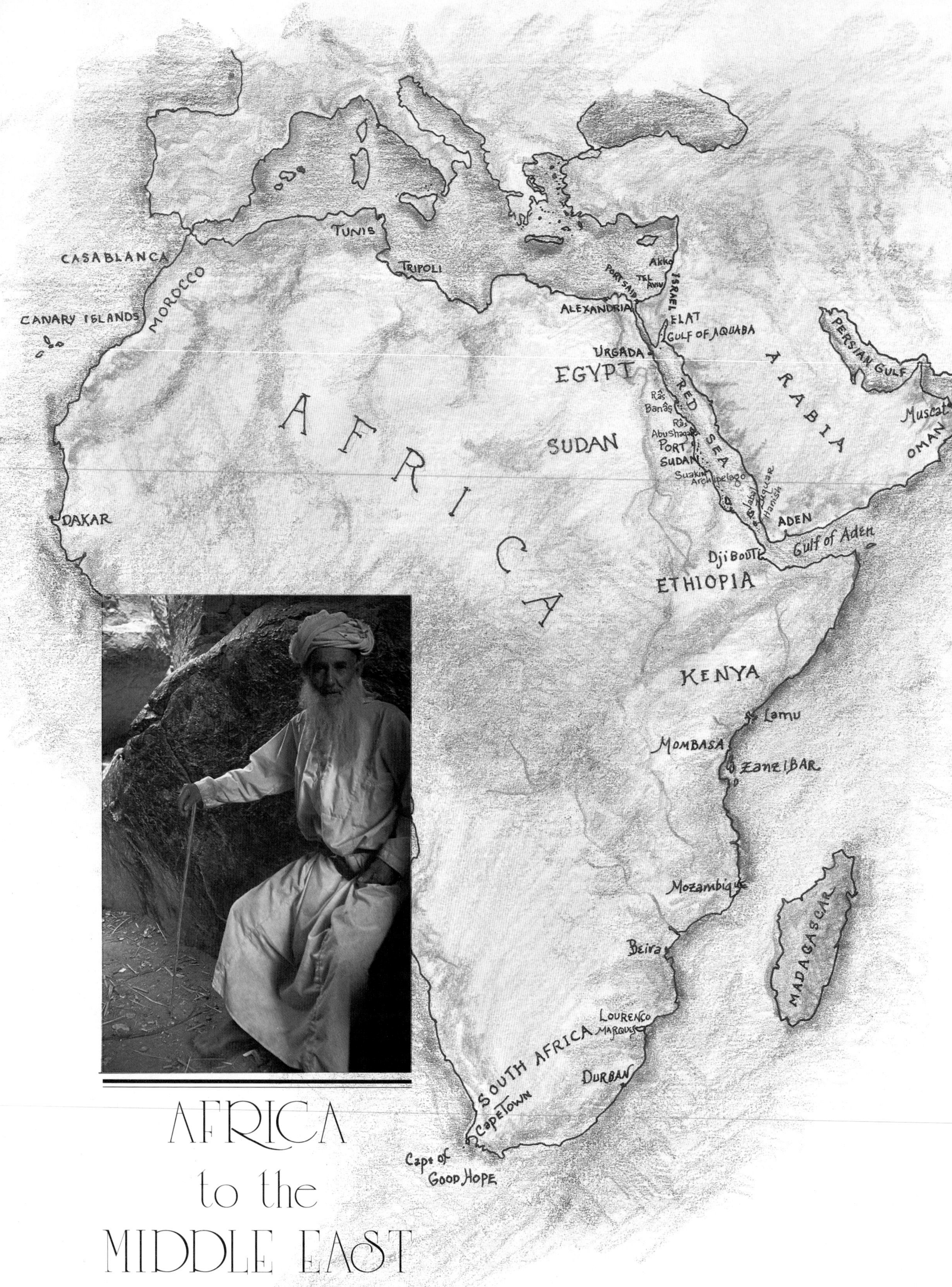

AFRICA to the MIDDLE EAST

WERNER BRAUN

ALAIN GUILLOU

A.

Good reviews were also given to Khor Inkeifal, opposite Mukawwar Island, and Khor Shin'Ab, north of the Ras Abu Shagara headland.

Entering Egyptian waters, Ras Banas, the headland above Foul Bay, offers good protection in all weather with splendid diving nearby.

Urgada, where the Red Sea constricts into the Gulf of Suez, can be a base for exploring the ancient wonders of the Valley of the Kings near Luxor. Nearby, there is an exceptional harbor in a fishhook-shaped bay — Endeavour anchorage, on Tawila Island. This lovely bay is protected from all directions and is close to good diving.

B.

WERNER BRAUN

A. Urgada Harbor, Egypt
B. Ancient harbor of Ceasarea
C. D. Akko, Israel

ISRAEL

The Phoenicians perfected sail power and navigation in 1100 B.C., then turned their trading skills voraciously outward. In addition to establishing colonies in Africa and Spain, these former residents of the Levant ventured to places in the Indian Ocean, including the fabled, and today undetermined, "Land of Ophir." The fleet that made these journeys was supposedly built in the port of Elat, at the head of the Gulf of Aquaba. Almost 3000 years later, this port in Israel is still launching and servicing voyages to adventure.

On the Mediterranean coast, the ancient Roman port of Caesarea was one of many of the harbor outposts of the Roman Empire that stretched from Britain to the Indian Ocean. It is reputed to have been a haven for those fishers of men, the disciples of Jesus Christ. It has silted in now, and harbors mainly history, and sailboarders.

Akko, the former Acre, is a living Israeli port with a long history. During medieval times, the Mediterranean was the axis of extensive world trade, extending from the Far East to the Baltic Sea. Constantinople, Antioch, Tripoli, and Acre were centers of exchange. In autonomous districts in each of these eastern ports, agents, or *factories* as they were called from the homeports of Venice, Genoa or Marseille, conducted business. Shipowners traded their goods and then carried them west into the Mediterranean homeports, which funneled the goods over the Alps into Europe. The discovery of the New World dispersed this power from the central coffers. Nonetheless, a great deal of trade passed through the eastern Mediterranean and Acre on its way across Suez.

Although the area is not a common destination for cruising sailors, there are many Israeli sailors, and good facilities. Many do stop to visit the Holy Land and to witness the metamorphosis that the Israelis have wrought. Pilgrims and tourists still throng to visit Jerusalem, Bethlehem, and the shrines. There seems to be a sacred stillness there, amidst the conflict.

WERNER BRAUN

C. D.

WERNER BRAUN

TURKISH RIVIERA

DANA JINKINS

THE MEDITERRANEAN

The snow-capped Taurus Mountains sweep down to the sea along the Turkish Riviera, a sunny corner of Anatolia where the Aegean meets the Mediterranean and East meets West. Palms and citrus groves fringe a myriad of small ports, coves and anchorages. Waterfalls tumble to the sea between beautiful white sand beaches and rocky promontories.

The coast of Anatolia could stand alone as an attractive cruising ground, offering the sailor a preponderance of good, safe, harbors with most amenities and services. The luxuriant foliage offers a refreshing change from some of the more arid Mediterranean shores. What further embellishes the Turkish Riviera, however, and surpasses the ordinary, is the exotic Oriental flavor of the place. Just a few steps past the Greek Islands, and more remote and less trodden, it seems an older world, incorporating vestiges of Islam and the Far East — the zeal of the jihad intermingled with the mystery of the Orient.

The procession of powerful and illustrious former inhabitants along this coast goes back to before the reign of Cleopatra. Mark Anthony bequeathed Cilicia (the region around Kas and Demre today) to her for a wedding gift. Southern Anatolia was settled by the Phoenicians, then by the pre-Hellenic tribes of the Mycenaeans, Pamphylians, Carians, and Lycians. We can credit the Lycians with the construction of most of the fabulous cities still in existence as archaeological sites here today. You can see where the Romans added their touch. You can also walk the same paths along the coast that the Ephesians, the Apostles, and the Virgin Mary walked. Barbarossa patrolled these waters six centuries ago during the era of the Ottoman Sultan's Empire. And the Crusaders built their castles everywhere. It is a fascinating place filled with eclectic remnants. The sequence of this historical parade becomes more clearly defined here than at other arenas of antiquities.

DANA JINKINS

A. B.

DANA JINKINS

C.

DANA JINKINS

DANA JINKINS

D.

Antalya is the principal port on the Turkish Riviera. It is a quiet, lovely port at the foot of the Old Town; its ramparts are adorned with minarets. Above to the north and west, the mountains appear to float like a cloud in a perpetually blue sky. A considerable flux of Turkish passenger ships share the breakwater, and vessels of international navies often lie offshore in the outer gulf.

Tiled arcades of Moorish arches stand next to wood and lath houses reminiscent of those in Northern Europe. Second-story bay windows protrude over the street. This is an architectural feature which was invented in Turkey to accommodate needs for space and privacy. Traditionally, the bay window was furnished with a blue sofa and embroideries within, and decorative tile and lath work without. Women in veils or white headscarves survey the street below from these eyries. The Gate of Hadrian stands in marble splendor at one edge of the Old Town, a souvenir of the reign of this Roman Emperor who ruled in 130 A.D.

E.

DANA JINKINS

A. Village of Ucagiz
B. Scarf merchants
C. Rug shop in Ucagiz
D. Harbor of Antalya
E. Turkish Gulets anchored in Antalya
Page 111: Ancient walls of Kekova

DANA JINKINS

A. B.

DANA JINKINS

Under the awnings and amongst the Persian rugs of the market square, a palpable feeling of the Orient is astir. Handsome smiling merchants — often richly adorned with embroideries, trinkets and headdresses — hawk the local crafts of silk and leather, rugs, textiles, silver, copper and spice. The rich provender of the coastal plain fills stalls with a colorful bounty of citrus, dates, bananas, cheeses, and all manner of greens. Livestock and tethered fowl add to the chaos. Huge bales of cotton, wool and woven kilims are stacked up in the cool dim interiors, around a little carpeted enclave of repose, from whence issues the aroma of incense. Serious shoppers might be invited into this inner sanctum to drink tea. Several times during the day, a carillon from the mosque calls the Moslem faithful to prayer.

Sailing west along the Lycian peninsula between Antalya and Fethiye are several delightful small modern-day ports, from which you can journey to a more magnificent harbor of millennia past. Near the excellent marina at Kemer is the ancient Rhodian port of Phaselis, dating back to 700 B.C. The three harbors are silted in now, but from the temples on the hill above, you can clearly see the colonnades and the aqueduct, delineating a fair-sized port. In contrast to the hot and dusty Pyramids and many other archaeological sites, a visit to the pine groves and palm glens of Phaselis is like a picnic.

On the slopes of Mount Olympus, just inland and 250 meters up, an eternal flame leaps out of the rock. This miraculous flame inspired the myth of the *Chimaera* and *Bellerophon* and is the sanctuary of the Roman Vulcan. This phenomenon is surrounded by ruins of many different eras. One of its interesting attributes is that even rain does not extinguish the flame; on the contrary, rain encourages the flame to grow stronger. This century it is mostly forgotten or merely dismissed as being derived from deposits of natural gas.

The pleasant, unpretentious fishing port of Finike offers access to some glorious national parks and the ruins of Myra, at Demre. One of the outstanding features of Lycian architecture is the elaborately carved rock tombs, usually

C.

D.

set impossibly high in a cliff face. The tombs at Myra are lower down, and offer the visitor the opportunity to examine the intricate carving at close range. The tombs resemble the homes and buildings of the departed souls, and often include porches, porticoes, and family portraits. The craftsmanship is truly remarkable. A vision of one or more of these tombs may suddenly appear in the hills, in Dalyan, for example, or the Gulf of Fethiye.

Relics of former civilizations adorn the land and sea all along this coast. A Turkish gentleman describes the island of Kekova:

"My favourite little place to anchor in the whole of the Aegean coast is Kekova. When you enter the bay you can stop over at a very small harbor in Kekova to your starboard side, see a beautiful Roman archway, and take a swim there. After your swim, take your boat across in front of Kalekoy,formerly Simena, a little fishing village.

As you enter the harbor, little children in boats selling hand-made headscarves will approach and, sometimes, a fisherman will offer you a big fish that he caught that morning. Anchor carefully and make reservations at one of the restaurants that traditionally serve fish. Then take your drinks and go up to the castle, which dates back to the Middle Ages, to watch the sunset.

The young children formerly went to school in the next village in unprotected boats, even in the winter. I decided to build a primary school there. It is situated beneath the castle and, if you go there, you will see it. Until recently, the village had no electricity or water and the restaurants, in order to light their ghastly neon signs and refrigerate the fish they serve and play oriental music, had to run generators which made the normally quiet bay very noisy until midnight. Now that electricity has been brought to the village, no generator noise is heard but, during the day, you can see TV aerials sticking out from the little houses.

Kalekoy (Simena) is one of those totally protected sites where you can only buy and restore existing buildings or ruins; no new building is allowed. The site is an old Lycian settlement with tombs all around; there is even one in the sea which gives the place a very quaint atmosphere. Should you dive (no scuba diving is permitted, you have to dive with a snorkel), you will see archaeological sites, amphoras and what-have-you on the seabed. That underwater sight alone is out of this world. I would advise snorklers not to collect anything from the seabed, as it is not permitted.

As for supplies, very small shops and markets have recently sprung up in Ucagiz village around the corner from Simena. The little Ucagiz (Teimussa or Tristamos) village is becoming lively,as pensions, restaurants, antique shops and gift shops open up.

If you have time you can go farther east about four or five miles to another bay and take a car from there to Demre (Myra), the famous birthplace of Santa Klaus. I would advise yachtsmen to see it if they have come as far south as Kekova."

Rahmi M. Koc
Yacht Owner / Istanbul, Turkey

A. Lycian tombs, Demre
B. Stone tomb, Kekova
C. Archeological detail
D. Amphitheatre, Demre

STEPHANIE BERKE

A.

Further to "Harbors of Enchantment" I nominate Kastellorizon, which is the most easterly Greek island close to the Turkish coast on the way to Cyprus. It remains a simple and beautiful port fortunately not developed, with the added advantage of a gigantic man-made stair path leading from the little village up over the mountain to a monastery, which can give any yacht person heart-wrenching exercise every morning scaling the heights. It may well be that someone can succeed in running up the stairs. I tried and failed, as did many youthful friends. On the other hand, there is no medical assistance so I do not recommend anyone to seriously try who isn't very fit.

There are a couple of small tavernas in town and some stunning abandoned 19th Century houses; legacies of when the population was 20,000. It is now sadly 2000, but exceedingly beautiful.

Jon

Jon Bannenberg
Yacht Designer
London, England

The island of Kastellorizon bears the lonely distinction of being the easternmost Greek island on the Turkish coast. Perhaps it should be in the chapter on Greece, but its lone star attributes are further corroborated by the fact that not only is it a Greek island among Turkish islands, but its feeling, architecture, and culture are distinctly Italian. The vicissitudes of its fortunes have left it sparsely inhabited, a veritable ghost town against the blue *Ak Deniz* (the Mediterranean Sea). It's a pleasant anchorage, with the spirits of pirates and princes in the wings.

Directly across the narrow strait, at Kas, the lively bohemian trekker's crowd has been augmented by a crew of diving archaeologists. The divers are in town to assist in the excavation of a Bronze Age shipwreck, which attests to a diversified mercantile trade in 1400 B.C., extending from Sardinia to the Middle East. There is a palpable feeling of excitement, discovery and life.

Some of the same wares are traded 3400 years later here in the markets of Kas and Kalkan. In the pastures and fields nearby, peasant women are handspinning fleece, as they did in centuries gone by. They produce the beautiful *kilims* for which Turkey has a continuing acclaim. The fleece is dyed and woven in clusters, in patterns distinctive to the villages of the weaver.

Turkey is still peopled by numerous gypsies and nomadic tribes. Those in southern Anatolia migrate, with their livestock and their belongings on camelback, from the mountain pastures in summer to the fertile coastal belt in winter. To come upon one of these encampments in a seaside grove of pines is an unforgettable experience. The tents erected, and camels tethered, these dark, beautiful people draped in brocades and jewelry, wearing all of their wealth, produce an exotic vision indeed.

A. Kastellorizon Harbor
B. Port of Kas
C. Anchorage at ruins of Knidos

B. C.

DANA JINKINS

DANA JINKINS

DANA JINKINS

LINDOS

The Acropolis, with its temple to Athena and medieval fortress, crowns an isthmus which separates the anchorage from the small-craft harbor of St. Paul. Tradition has it that the apostle himself landed here on a missionary journey. Stands of cypress trees and ornate villas mingle on the slopes of the Acropolis, along with tidy whitewashed houses stacked like cubes. This vision recedes down to the bay which resembles an amphitheater surrounded by olive groves. Against the stunning background, yachts and *caiques* swing at anchor in turquoise waters against an arc of beach.

SYMI

Sailing into the deep, narrow harbor of Symi, set between steep hillsides, I was profoundly struck by the quiet beauty of the place. Its perfect little harbor is punctuated to the north by a pretty campanile, below which sits a string of proud houses at the foot of a barren slope. They appear stark and vacant, but sudden bursts of noise and curtains fluttering out windows dispel that notion. Ghosts and saints seem to hover in the rigging of the *caiques* and around the silhouettes of the monasteries on high.

Symi's heyday occurred during Italian hegemony. Lack of soil and land resources produced a bounty of knowledgeable seamen; ultimately,Symi became a center for trade and pilotage. After entering the harbor, we tied up along the wharf next to a sponge diver in a sturdy and colorful craft. He was cleaning a sizeable catch of sponges on the thwarts of his little boat. Down the quay, an *arpeggio* of Italian chatter and laughter rang out from a sleek white yawl. Pungent scents of grilling fish and *calamari* wafted from the *taverna* at the foot of the gangplank. Here on the wharf the town breathes life.

Under the brilliant sky the stacked-up yellow houses with their red-tiled roofs encircled us. Many looked empty. I elected to take a walk before lunch.

A periphery of shops and the hub of village activity surround the harbor, but the farther up the hill you go, the fewer people you see. Goats and chickens graze in the terraced dusty paddocks, and blossoming oleander and bougainvillea poke out through old masonry. There is a trail of fallen houses along the way and then life starts up again. In the shade of doorsteps and arbors, and inside curtained windows, old women in black peruse the passers-by.

This strenuous climb is well worth the effort. Pockets of humanity live and thrive up here with clotheslines, children, and the murmur and clink of the corner *taverna* as proof. Between houses you glimpse an ever-broadening view of the harbor sparkling below.

THOMAS KAUL

A. B.

ROE ANNE WHITE

C.

Several coasting *caiques* have moored perpendicular to our boat on the seawall. The other side of the narrow harbor is so close, a mere kilometer away, and is a mirror image of this slope.

The walk could continue over the hill to the monastery, but I decided to sail there later. The other harbor on Symi is virtually a shrine to Agia Panormitis. This small bay lies to the northeast of the main harbor. Against the relentless stony poverty of Symi, this verdant bay, with its tranquil monastery shaded by pine and cypress trees appears serene and spiritual.

ROE ANNE WHITE

PATMOS

The port of Hora on the island of Patmos is a cloistered harbor that provides entry to a holy shore. Three volcanic islets close rank around the peaceful and beautiful port which sheltered the ships of the Apostle John, and those of many penitents and pilgrims who have flocked to the monastery in the centuries since. High above the village, on the way to heaven, St.John the Divine was meditating in a cave when he received the terrifying dreams which inspired his account of the Apocalypse. A monastery was founded on the site in the 11th century, and it has been a Christian shrine ever since.

A. Overview of Symi Harbor
B. Waterfront, Symi
C. Old Salt
D. Young Salt
E. Waterfront, Patmos
F. Harbor of Patmos

DANA JINKINS

D.

BILL ROBINSON

E.

F.

JEANETTE PHILLIPPS

Trieste
Venice
Brioni
YUGOSLAVIA
FIRENZA
ITALY
Zadar
Skradin
Split
Sibenik
Portofino
Santa Margherita
Viareggio
Korcula
Hvar
Dubrovnik
Elba
CORSICA
ROME
Bonifacio
Porto Cervo
COSTA SMERALDA
Ponza
Palmarola
Procida
Naples
Brindisi
Ischia
Sorrento
Capri
Positano
Amalfi
SARDINIA
Cagliari
Stromboli
Ustica
Palermo
Lipari
Panarea
Vulcano
Egadi Islands
Taormina
SICILY
Straits of Messina
Siracusa

ITALY

DANA JINKINS

VENICE

It's a long sail up the Adriatic, a fact which might explain why cruising sailors have all but forgotten this enchanting harbor. Several empires were launched here, and centuries of wealth have created an architectural gem. Venice is wound around canals and bridges, and serviced by a resplendent fleet of water transport.

Though its canals are surely polluted, and the island is rumored to be sinking under the weight of all this civilization, no one can deny the captivating charm of this city.

The marina on the island of San Giorgio Maggiore provides a perfect berth facing the Piazza San Marco, across the Grand Canal. You can sit in the Cafe Florian and sip the elixir of bygone splendor as you regard the ornate exuberance of the Cathedral and the Palace of the Doges. The languid waters, and the visual delights across canals and bridges, invite strolling and

Living in front of Piazza San Marco is a privilege which cannot be bought with money. The few ancient "Palazzi" belong strictly to the Venetian aristocracy, but yachts can moor tight to them. You can reach Cipriani, Harry's Bar, Piazza San Marco and the most beautiful shops, hotels and restaurants with your dinghy. Nowhere else in the world, can you anchor your boat right in the heart of such a city! And imagine, you are mooring your boat where the galleys moored 1000 years ago.

CARLO

Carlo Gandini
Italian Publisher/ Yacht Owner

ALAIN GUILLOU

ALAIN GUILLOU

DANA JINKINS

farniente (the divine act of doing nothing). Enticing aromas enroute will summon you to dine. Culinary excellence is another attribute of this sensuous city. The gourmand can scarcely go wrong here.

Exploring the cobbled streets and narrow passageways of Venice, or meandering the canals by gondola, dinghy, mahogany water-taxi or *vapore* are rewarding activities that provide an architectural feast. The grand old buildings house exquisite collections of Italian masters, as well as other styles of art. The churches alone are galleries without equal. The modern collections of wearable art are quite alluring, too, in this voluptuous setting where the human parade is especially rich. Venetian carnival is ever-present. There are an inordinate number of enticing shops filled with masks and costumes.

Venice built the fortresses that still guard the Mediterranean from Gibraltar to the Levant. Most rewarding to the sailor who has perambulated this expanse, and seen the architectural samples of the Venetian empire far and wide, is to visit the resplendent city that is the source.

Culture aside, Venice remains the most romantic city in the world!

DANA JINKINS

STEFANO NAVARRINI

A.

B.

SICILY

The populous tribe of Sicilians has grown and prospered under Mount Etna, the volcano that periodically erupts. Many live close to the land and sea, and appear more rustic and pastoral than their cousins who have emigrated to cities in America.

Mount Etna, a natural monument that rises to 11,000 feet, has wrought much destruction on the people of Sicily. Between eruptions, its fertile slopes host a cornucopia of fruit trees and vineyards as well as ski resorts.

The island has always been heavily populated, regardless of the volcanic menace. Relics of lost civilizations are abundant. Sicily contains a treasure horde of archaeological sites, dating back to Magna Graecia, Rome and the Saracens.

The ancient port of Syracuse merits a visit. The Old City decorates an islet with Moorish and Baroque architecture, and the port lies between it and the Sicilian mainland. Syracuse is crowned by a large and well-preserved Greek Theatre, dating from the fifth century B.C. The view of the city and the bay from here is superb.

JEANETTE PHILLIPPS

The Egadi Islands, off the western tip of Sicily, are the lonesome preserve of the sailor, the fisherman and wild goats. Fishermen and divers have discovered this quiet sanctuary, and luxuriate in an undersea world that is abnormally rich for the Mediterranean. Favignana is a quiet port guarded by old fortresses.

A. Levanzo, Sicily
B. Porto Piccola, Siracusa, Sicily
C. 16th century Norman castle, Lipari
D. The volcano of Stromboli
E. A fan of fishing boats, Stromboli

AEOLIAN ISLANDS

The Aeolian Islands are named for the god of wind and enshrine an active cone of fire. They are cast like jewels off Sicily where the straits of Messina usher into the Tyhrrenian Sea. Whirlpools and volcanoes aside, this region has been the locus of manmade history for at least 4000 years. The *mistral* (godly wind) brings autumn rains and the sun shines throughout the winter creating the renowned floral beauty in these islands .

Stromboli is continually letting off steam in spectacular bursts of fire and ash; blazing streams of lava are visible at night. Vulcanologists claim that this venting process, as in human nature, will prevent a cataclysmic eruption. Built on faith in this theory, several tiny villages cluster along the beach on the leeward side of the perfect cone. This side is innocuous enough, with rolling green slopes, vines and shrubbery. The western slope, however, is grim, cold and lifeless — desolate flanks of spilled black and red ash. If all this geothermal fury inspires a desire for catharsis, the island of Vulcano offers sulphur steams and relaxing hot mud baths.

The tiny port of Panarea is the jewel of them all. Europe's *glitterati* on their opulent yachts crowd into the tiny harbor alongside the launches and fishing boats of locals. Even the jet-set is attracted by this port's seclusion and simplicity so gracefully adorned and perfumed by an amazing diversity of flora. "Islomania" seems to be a common denominator among sailors, probably their main inspiration for going to sea. Panarea has what islomaniacs need.

STEFANO NAVARRINI

C. D.

ROE ANNE WHITE

E.

STEFANO NAVARRINI

PREBEN NYELAND

A. B.

BILL ROBINSON

SARDINIA

Sardinia is a glorious, wild island with a long history and a unique development. Ruins near Barumini date from the Bronze Age, and the conical stone towers called *nuraghe*, found only on Sardinia, have a mystical quality. They are estimated to be 3000 years old. The Sardinians are historically an insular people, non-seafaring, and hence their cultural development has been totally different from that of the Mediterranean mainland. The Sardinians were shepherds, and the coasts have remained largely undeveloped through the centuries.

In the seventies, a consortium, including the Aga Khan, discovered the Costa Smeralda (the Emerald Coast), a spectacular region on the northeast cape. The shepherds had eschewed the rugged rock formations and wind battered cliffs that intersect the beaches and turquoise lagoons, so there was nothing, not even a fishing village, there twenty years ago.

The group designed and invented Porto Cervo and community to accommodate Europe's wandering wealthy, who are perpetually seeking a holiday roost. There are many small coves and fine hotels, but Cala di Volpe stands out as the most exceptional. The architecture around Porto Cervo is Sardo-Moorish and all construction must conform. This planned development sounds too organized, but in reality, it is quite beautiful and really works. The marine facilities have become the base for many sailing races: offshore powerboats, 12-meters, Swans, Maxis and classic yacht regattas. Porto Cervo is also summer headquarters for some of Europe's most splendid yachts. There is a shipyard capable of hauling eight 12-meter racers at once. Many race boats turn up here after different cup races to repair and recuperate.

In the past few decades, the island of shepherds has leapt from a pastoral economy to a booming industry in tourism, as well as in mines and manufacturing. The natives maintain their unique and colorful traditions, and apparently have initiated a cautious plan for development. The tourism hub, so far, is mostly limited to the Costa Smeralda; in any case, the furor is all so recent that it is still common to see the traditional festivals. Sardinian embroideries and other ceremonial garments are exquisite. Their hospitality is legendary.

C.

D.

DANA JINKINS

A. Aerial view of Porto Cervo
B. Cala di Volpe
C. Sardo-Moorish architecture, Porto Cervo
D. Dinghy dock

Porto Cervo, pronounced "chervo", is a beautiful playground carved out of a rather desolate area of northern Sardinia called Costa Smeralda, or "Emerald Coast," aptly named for the clear green water there. The Aga Khan and a number of his friends bought the land and spearheaded development of the coast. With strict architectural rules and guidelines in effect during construction all the private and commercial properties blend in to an aesthetically pleasing, old-world charm. The centerpiece is the modern harbor with its gem of a yacht club, one of the most beautiful I've seen anywhere in the world. Every modern yachting convenience is right at hand, yet you can sail a mile away to a quiet harbor with a white sandy beach for lunch.

Hotels abound, but blend in with the surroundings. We stayed at Cala di Volpe during one maxi-yacht series I was sailing in, and then we stayed at Luci di la Montagna during the Swan World's Championships. The former is one of the best hotels along the coast with excellent food and charming rooms - very expensive. The latter is more modest, centrally located, and overlooks the harbor, yet is clean and quiet.

If you have a chance to go to Porto Cervo, don't miss it.

Stephen Colgate
Chief Executive Officer / Offshore Sailing School Ltd.

STEFANO NAVARRINI

A.

B.

STEFANO NAVARRINI

C.

BARRY BAILEY

RIDI

D.

A. Palmarola, Pontine Archipelago
B. Ventotene
C. An anchorage on Ponza
D. Aerial view of the old harbor, Portoferraio, Elba

Elba has been inhabited since prehistoric times with relics dating back 50,000 years. It was the crossroad of Phoenicians, Etruscans, Greeks, Romans and Carthagenese. The Greeks used to call it "Aethalia." Ancient writers tell that Jason and the Argonauts stopped here to repair their boats during their epic navigation. The Etruscans excavated the fabulous iron mines which provided great riches to the island, until recent years when they were abandoned in favor of tourism.

From the Middle Ages on, Pisa, Genova, Florence, Spain and France fought over Elba and regularly the island was raided by Saracen pirates (among them the infamous Barbarossa, "Red Beard"). In 1803 Elba became part of France. In 1814 Napoleon was forced to abdicate and exiled to Elba. The emperor who directed the destiny of Europe for so long was nominated "King of Elba." In the few months he lived there he organized the island, built roads, unified the different communes of Elba, developed the mines, all in a way to try to make the island as independent as possible. His spirit is still alive in Elba. In 1860 Elba was attached to the United Kingdom of Italy.

Portoferraio (Iron Harbor) was described by Admiral Nelson as one of the most perfect natural harbors in the world. The bay is huge, beautiful, and protected in all kinds of weather; definitely the best bay on this side of the Mediterranean.

The old harbor is surrounded by the impressive fortifications of the Medicis built on medieval walls, which had themselves been constructed on Roman and Etruscan relics. It is a very colorful town, full of life, with narrow streets and stairways leading to the forts and the walls.

On the west side of the bay is the modern harbor, where ferries arrive from the continent. There are several boat yards where all kinds of facilities, repairs, water and fuel are available.

Elba has two other harbors. Porto Azurro on the southeast side of the island offers protection from the mistral. On the northwest is another nice little harbor and the charming town of Marciana Marina. The many indentations of the island offer several nice anchorages, beautiful beaches and a varied landscape. The population is friendly and hospitable, and the food is very good; as elsewhere in Italy the cuisine is based mostly on seafood, and there are nice local wines. The island is most beautiful in spring time when everything is in bloom before the rush of the summer.

Nicole

Nicole Peraud Zaccagni
Sailor/ Gourmet Chef/ Traveler

ITALIAN TOURIST BOARD

A. B. C.

RIDI

RIDI

THE ITALIAN RIVIERA

Portofino, the pearl of the Ligurian Riviera, came by her distinction as a harbor of enchantment in the old-fashioned way — she earned it. This delightful little port at the head of a tiny inlet is surprisingly deep and perfectly protected. It has been the haven of seafarers since time immemorial. The Romans christened it *Porto Delphini,* (the Port of Dolphins) from which the present name is derived. Many of the lovely tall ochre-colored houses that surround the port date from the time of the Crusades; the Portofinese were valiant navigators, seagoing merchants and crusaders themselves.

It is a tiny place, located at the outward extremity of a rugged peninsula and a twisting narrow road, under Monte Portofino. Only about 800 people live there, but the whole glittering world comes to call. The Grand Hotel Splendido became famous as an international trysting spot for lovers, particularly from Hollywood. It is truly a romantic setting, with the scents of oleander and rosemary enhancing the perfect seascape.

Arrival by sea is definitely the preferred approach to Portofino, where space, parking and patience for day trippers is limited. Besides, the main orientation of the Portofinese is the sea; their lives are comprised of fishing, sailing and dining magnificently from the sea. A stroll to the lighthouse at twilight via the little Church of Saint George reveals one miraculous view after another — creeks tumbling through olive groves and on through pine trees, glimpses of villas high above and La Spezia afar and, from the lighthouse, the Gulf of Rapallo opens to view, with its waters caressing the bulwarks of this tight little haven.

A. Santa Margarita, Ligurian Riviera
B. Porto Ferraio, Elba
C. Porto Azzuro, Elba
D. E. Portofino

PHILLIP BOMMER

D.

E.

DANA JINKINS

CÔTE d'AZUR & CORSICA

COMPLIMENTS OF PRINCE RAINIER

A.

The Bay of Hercules has been for centuries a natural shelter for Mediterranean navigators until it was made into the harbour as it is today alas, open to the Easterly winds and swells!

Here, my great-grandfather, Prince Albert I (1848-1922) used to moor his frail schooner of 220 tons powered only by sail — the Hirondelle I (with which he made his first scientific cruises).

In 1891, encouraged by the scientific results obtained with such simple means, he had a ship designed and built especially for ocean work and equipped with an auxiliary 300 h.p. engine: the Princess Alice I.

In 1889, the Princess Alice II, a more powerful and better equipped ship aboard which Prince Albert explored the Arctic Seas as far north as Spitzberg, often returned to this harbour.

Albert I finally brought the series of cruises to an end - having always used the Monaco Harbour as a base - with the Hirondelle II, an elegant steel ship of 1650 tons with 2000 h.p. engines, and equipped with the most up-to-date laboratories and scientific equipment. Oceanography had become a true science!

Today, the most beautiful, sophisticated, private yachts have elected to stay in the harbour of Monaco as their favourite anchorage. Also, medium tonnage cruise ships make their stops in the harbour, adding a most appreciated extra activity.

All this has led us to study a project to increase the harbour's mooring capacity in calm waters. Part of Monaco's vocation - we must not forget - is tourism from the sea!

Prince Rainier of Monaco

Page 163**: **S/Y Puritan framed by the topsails of S/Y Shenandoah

THE RIVIERA

Images of the Riviera persist from my childhood, where soaring Alps rise to a cobalt heaven, shielding the shining beaches from the winter's wind, and medieval villages perch on cliffs, with trails of cypress winding down to azure seas. Gypsies, and maidens, and swanks from smart Paris walked down these paths and peopled my warm imaginings on a cheerless winter day in Minnesota.

It was under the sailpower of a cold *mistral*, some years later, that I caught my first glimpse of the Côte d'Azur — and it was all true! In the ionized clarity that comes after a cleansing storm, I could see what all the rapture was about. The rosy cliffs of the Esterel massif looked positively celestial; the cypresses were there, and the little pastel port of Agay wandered into a pinewoods that scrabbled upward to those alpine villages of my dreams.

It is truly a sublime and sensual landscape; small wonder the Riviera became the *locus extraordinaire* of international vacationers.

MONTE CARLO

It's a mundane world, and princes and fairy kingdoms are few and far between. Here on the Riviera, a principality flourishes, sheltered from the harsh winds of taxes and the storms of politics by an unusual royal ascendancy and a shoulder of mountain range.

This royal domain, less than one mile square, survives from the days of fiefdoms and duchies and all those minor hierarchies that seem so much more manageable than unwieldy and disparate nations. The Grimaldi clan bought Monte Carlo from the Genoese back in the 13th century, some of whom continue to lay claim to the wealth of the principality. The vicissitudes of its fortunes fluctuated through the centuries with internecine conflicts and aggression from abroad, but fiscal salvation came in the 1860s with the gambling excesses of one particularly impoverished scamp of a prince. To increase revenues, he initiated the informal gaming tables which eventually blossomed into casinos. The libertine atmosphere of the casinos complemented the restorative benefits of sunshine and the sea, and the tiny nation became a kingdom of pleasure.

There are many lovely hotels and resorts, but the magnificent Hermitage Hotel and the gracious Hotel de Paris make the fairytale quality of Monte Carlo complete. Sitting on the terrace of the Hotel de Paris, with a wandering violinist serenading, you can watch the procession of Porsches and Ferraris pull up to the Grand Casino. This small monarchy is full of sculpted gardens, grottoes, museums and many attractions, not the least of which is the Prince's Palace. Artists, musicians, gypsies, race car drivers, businessmen, gamblers, and sailors all convene here for *divertissement*. Monte Carlo is a show, and some of the star features are on parade in the harbor. The fabulous yachts of the world's wealthy gleam perennially in the Bay of Hercules.

A. Monte Carlo Harbor circa 1906
B. Modern day Monte Carlo
C. The Grand Casino, Monte Carlo
D. Old salt

DANA JINKINS

B.

C.

DANA JINKINS

D.

DANA JINKINS

ANTIBES

The port of Antibes with its acres of masts is a trifle too crowded to truly be an enchanting harbor. However, it is a mecca for so many yachts that there has to be a reason for them to gather there.

The port is more than a marine facility; it is a self-proclaimed yachting center or club of cruising sailors on their way somewhere else. Crews can provision from a wide variety of market produce, and spare parts are available; dockside socializing is a constant, and numerous yacht brokers will promise to sell your boat or find you a new one. Boats of every persuasion show up in Antibes. Recently, a large boat quay behind the breakwater was built to accommodate the current proliferation of mega-yachts.

Always a coastal port of call, the Greeks set up trading posts in Antibes in the fourth century B.C. They were succeeded by the Romans and then the Barbarians. More recent history speaks of Napoleon leaving his family in Antibes while he defended the coast. And after the fall of Robespierre, Napoleon was imprisoned at Fort Carré. The 16th century fort is still existent. Also noteworthy in the Old Town are the Grimaldi Castle and the Picasso Museum.

Just a few miles away nestled in the hills is the village of Grasse. The essences produced here are the base material for the Parisian perfume industry. Traveling through the winding streets of Grasse, bouquets of lavender, jasmine and tea rose can be purchased among the many essences. Winds blow through the highlands and import these fragrant aromas down to the Riviera.

DANA JINKINS.

A. B.

DANA JINKINS

A. B. St. Paul de Vence
C. View of Cannes Harbor from the spreaders of S/Y Shenandoah
D. Old Town, Cannes
E. M/Y Carinthia VI

DANA JINKINS

C. D.

FRENCH GOV'T. TOURIST OFFICE

E.

DANA JINKINS

CANNES

Guy de Maupassant anchored in Cannes Harbor and was so impressed with the anchorage and the sheer red cliffs of the Corniche de l'Esterel (the heights of Esterel) that he was moved to write about this town in his book, *On the Water*. The natural allure of Cannes was first discovered by painters, followed by filmmakers and their stars and fans, and today the annual Cannes Film Festival is considered *de rigeur* for anyone connected to international *avant garde* cinema.

Cannes is a glittering panorama by night and day, especially when viewed from the sanctuary of your cockpit. Many earthly pleasures and tantalizing attractions attend the surreal excursion ashore.

In contrast to the hustle of the urban Riviera, take a trip inland to the ravines and villages of the Esterel massif. These porphyritic mountains near Cap Roux have a pinkish cast, and are striated with other vivid colors. Every turn presents incomparable views, and the air is invigorating. Natural highs on the trails can then be rewarded with a repast in one of the quixotic villages tucked in these mountain eyries.

ST. TROPEZ

The port of St. Tropez is perhaps the apotheosis of the Riviera town. Sharing all the natural attributes of the aforementioned resorts, it started out as an artists' colony in the thirties, attracting painters with international reputations as well as luminaries from the Parisian *literati*. Set on the south shore of one of the most splendid bays on the Riviera, the port looks out from under the slopes of a citadel, which hosts a musical festival each summer.

The pastel buildings that line the quays house cafés and cabarets. The entire village creates a stage-set atmosphere for a captivating and continually changing parade of characters.

The yachts of the rich and famous have always turned up in St. Tropez. The dazzling vision of floating empires, the latest in ocean racers, and the rigging of grand old sailing ships add color to the street scene, literally a leap away from the bow of your vessel.

DANA JINKINS

A.

B.

ALAIN GUILLOU

PORQUEROLLES

Off the coast of Hyères is a group of small islands, the north face of which offers a view of the Côte d'Azur from sandy beaches, fragrant pine glens and rolling vineyards. The southern coast turns a stony shoulder of glinting mica to the Mediterranean; hence their name L'Îles d'Or, "islands of gold."

The commotion of motorcars and the mania to be chic are a mere few miles away on the Riviera, but there are no such perturbations on Les Isles d'Hyères. On Porquerolles, the larger island, the pretty little port town has an amiable insouciance and enough terraced cafés and restaurants to attend you, without all the boggling choices and crowds of other resorts in these purlieus. The wooded interior is undeveloped and likely to remain a natural preserve protected by the state. Its gently-trampled footpaths and shady lanes meander through olive groves, vineyards, eucalyptus and lavender.

The southern shore has some secluded anchorages where nests of pine needles and olive shade have taken root between the craggy headlands — private, romantic retreats for those so inclined. These islands, especially Port Cros, are rich in the French literature of love. Levant, the island where the sun rises, is the home of a celebrated nudist colony, Heliopolis.

This archipelago seems to have had a magnetic appeal for a diversified collection of people, whether for romance, military strategy or hermitage. The islands were Greek and Roman outposts before they became the fifth century refuge of Lerin monks. The perverse notion that many rulers shared, to populate colonies with prisoners, backfired on King Francois who granted asylum and immunity to criminals as long as they stayed on the Iles d'Hyères. Apparently, crooks and felons happily flocked to the islands, and the archipelago became the lair of pirates and *malfaiteurs* (outlaws) for centuries.

A. Sunset stroll, St. Tropez waterfront
B. Aerial view of St. Tropez harbor
C. Sunset over Porquerolles

MICHELE DARD

C.

Porquerolles, an island seven kilometers by three kilometers is situated in the bay of Hyères. The anchorage in the harbour is sheltered from eastwinds; when the Mistral blows it is better to be tied up at the docks of the marina. From the yacht club, there is a very good view of the harbour. If you arrive at Regatta time, the second week of May for "Porquerolles Cup," and the first week of September for the "Full Moon Regatta," you will find it a good occasion to taste the famous rosé wine produced by Sebastian Leber, "the active commodore". The natives love wooden boats and world-sailing yachts.

Ashore, there are few cars, but lots of bicycles, and from the steps of the "Mexican-looking church" in the small village square you can watch the locals playing "boules," and feel the atmosphere that makes this stop very special.

Natalie
Natalie Guillaume
French cruising sailor/ entrepreneur

CORSICA

Corsica, a spiritual child, but never a willing subject, of the French *République* was a province of the Genoese for 400 years; they constructed the citadels and many towers that circumscribe the periphery. The Corsicans have always been proud, and rebelled repeatedly for their independence; they finally succeeded in ridding themselves of the Genoese in 1769 and were overtaken by France. Napoleon was born there the year that Corsica joined the French nation.

The Corsicans are a rich and complex people with elements of Arabic spice and Mediterranean high color in their culture as well as their cuisine. Corsican olive oil is some of the best in the world.

At the very southern tip of the island is Bonifacio, isolated by the sea on one side and desert land on the other. The port is formidable because the very nature of the landscape is rock-girt and like a fortress. History has marched through here, and left its traces of Napoleon. The cemetery of Bonifacio, the Campo Santo, is a miniature city of the dead, where tombs mimic houses looking out to sea. Calvi is a charming and less formidable harbor on the northwest coast. Sprawling fig trees shade the ramparts and arches around town.

BARRY BAILEY

A.

B.

ROE ANNE WHITE

C.

JOHN DONOVAN

STEPHANIE BERKE

D.

E.

STEPHANIE BERKE

A. Yachts moored in the Straits of Bonifacio
B. Watchtowers on a rock fortress
C. Port of Bonifacio
D. Port of Calvi, Corsica
E. Bustling port of Bonifacio

JEANETTE PHILLIPPS

A.

B.

WESTERN MEDITERRANEAN

For millennia, the Mediterranean Sea has been a nerve center and a generator for far-flung trade. Commerce and piracy, wars and crusades, embarkations to discovery and romance have been carried out here, acts that have greatly influenced the comtemporary character of these islands in its midst. It is like a boiling cauldron containing cultures of many shores, with transients thrown in as added spice, and then the entire contents poured agresively upon neighboring shores. Islands caught in the stream of this ethnic maelstrom have developed some of the most acute passions, and colorful ports.

ROE ANNE WHITE

MALTA

My first glimpse of Malta was landfall in a rosy golden dawn, the honey-gilt battlements rising above the horizon like a vision out of "The Arabian Nights." The architecture is Moorish, with brushstrokes of English influence as seen in the pubs proffering pints of bitter, the green grocers, chandlers and ships stores. Centuries of ministering to maritime fleets under many flags have left their mark. From the Crusaders to the Allies in World War II, mariners came to Valletta, Malta for repair and refuge because of its convenient location in the middle of the Mediterranean.

The three small islands comprising Malta are densely populated, and though the Arabic and British influence is more overt, the multifarious cultures of the Phoenicians, Carthaginians, Romans, Byzantines, Normans, Knights of St. John and French have contributed to the melting pot. The Maltese language is predominantly of Semitic/Arabic origin, coupled with a strong dose of Latin and a smattering of British expressions to complete the strange blend.

The Knights of Malta and the Maltese falcon have brought world-wide recognition to this small nation. The island was granted to the Knights in fief by Charles V of Spain in 1530 after they had been ousted from Rhodes by Ottoman Turks. Though Malta was not an impressive property when the Knights arrived, they couldn't complain about the price: one falcon on All Saints' Day of each year.

A military and hospital order, the Knights had to be of noble birth. Most came from Aragon, France, Germany, Provence, Castile, Auvergne and Italy. Being as adept at building as at soldiering, they graced the islands with beautiful structures representing the styles of their homelands.

A. Maltese fishing boats
B. Harbor of Valletta, Malta
C. Colorful Maltese craft
D. Ruins at Mnajdra
page 175: Lagoon at Andraitx, Majorca

JEANETTE PHILLIPPS

C.

D.

JEANETTE PHILLIPPS

JIM JUDD

A.

B.

JEANETTE PHILLIPPS

C.

JEANETTE PHILLIPPS

The Maltese falcon, introduced to the world in the Humphrey Bogart movie, is no more. Malta is infested with bird hunters who shoot prodigious numbers of migratory birds for fun. A pair of peregrine falcons were nesting on cliffs in Malta as recently as two years ago, but they were shot.

Resort hotels are in abundance here, and a strong emphasis is placed on tourism. Recreational beaches are few, however, and often crowded, but that probably won't deter the million visitors expected next year. For those with an historical bent, the ruins at Hagar Qim, Tarxien and Gozo are interesting to explore. They house over 30 temples that are among the world's oldest stone monuments.

The North African coast was the home of the Barbary pirates. They gained political significance when they grafted their powers of piracy onto the merchant class of the Ottoman Empire, in order to enrich the coffers of the sultans of Algeria and Tunis.

Barbarossa, for instance, led several military maneuvers against the Christian battalions, which resulted in the Turks acquiring the Eastern Mediterranean. The menace of the Barbary pirates existed for three centuries after the death of Barbarossa, well into modern-day memory, and the folklore surrounding these swarthy *malfaiteurs* figures abundantly in the history of all the Mediterranean Islands.

Carthage, in the Gulf of Tunis, was prominent in the Barbary sagas. The land mass that protected Carthage has eroded now, and tearooms and train tracks have been laid over its ruins. A new breakwater at Sidi Bou Said offers shelter below the Old City, and land transport to Tunis. Bizerte is also a fascinating natural harbor in the midst of a bustling North African city. The city is built along a channel between Lake Banzart and the coast.

ROE ANNE WHITE

D.

E.

A.G.E. FOTOSTOCK

A. Fishing fleet at Essouira, Morocco
B. Harbor of Bizerte, Tunisia
C. Harbor canal in Bizerte
D. Sunset in the Balearics
E. Puerto Soller, Majorca

D.

THE BALEARIC ISLANDS

Strategically located as a stepping stone in the mid-Mediterranean and a marine outpost for launching maneuvers and repairs, the Balearic Islands have witnessed a fabulous historical pageant over the years. Ibiza and Formentera, Majorca and Menorca were the scene of conquests and occupation by a host of civilizations on their way to somewhere. Carthaginians, Greeks, Romans and Huns were the first occupants, followed by a myriad of others, including the noble race of tourists.

Under the crown of Aragon, the kingdom of Majorca included the Balearic Islands and the Catalan Coast as far as the Auvergne. Newly liberated from the constraints of Islam, and not yet repressed by those of the Christian Empire, these islands were flourishing, along with Languedoc, Perpignan and Montpellier, as an independent and spirited kingdom. It was during this time that the inhabitants developed great skills in cartography and navigation as well as in literature. They wrote in the dialect of the mainland Catalan which distinguishes them today.

KLAUS ALVERMANN

A.

B.

ROE ANNE WHITE

helped the natives to maximize their agriculture. These ancient windmills still grace the island.

The rocky islet of Vedra is yet another place which claims to be the mythical home of Ulysses' sirens. If you feel drawn to explore them, local fishing boats can give you a lift. Wonderful hikes can be made to Atalaya Peak, and excursions to the villages of outland Ibiza. Witches are said to inhabit Formentera, an island neighbor worthy of a visit. If not Ulysses, Ibiza does have some ghosts from an eventful past.

A. Salt works of Ibiza
B. Citadel, Ibiza
C. Barcelona waterfront
D. Peñon de Ifach, Calpe

MEDITERRANEAN SPAIN

The archetypal seat of Catalan autonomy and much of its political and intellectual heart is in Barcelona. Like a phoenix, this fascinating city has fallen and risen many times; it is currently undergoing another metamorphosis to receive the world in the next Olympic Games. It does not have a sterling harbor, but the Barcelonians are currently renewing marina facilities. The cultural attributes definitely merit a visit while on this coast.

Among other invasions, the Costa del Sol has long been the holiday destination of hordes of Northern Europeans; consequently, skyscraper hotels are flourishing in some of the formerly enchanted harbors, as well as all the pros and cons of a modest expatriate community. No holds seem to be barred now; the Spaniards are joining the holiday force with great gusto. After the repression of the Franco years, exuberance seems to be the order of the day.

The city of Alicante is a wonderful old town with a graceful esplanade. Its harbor is bustling with commercial traffic and is convenient to the markets and heart of the city. On either side of Cabo de la Nao are two quieter havens. Javea and Calpe are fishing harbors that have attracted a substantial expatriate land-based community. They offer good protection with full services and easy transport to Alicante.

Alicante, Valencia, Almeria, and Malaga are adequate harbors. For more exclusive service and ambiance on this coast, there is Puerto José Banus, a model marina and resort complex which offers a full spectrum of yachting needs.

Sevilla is an inland port on the Guadalquivir Estuary, 50 miles up the river from the Mediterranean. The Romans dredged the river, then made it the capital of Muslim Spain. Perhaps Sevilla's finest moment was in the 16th century, when discovery fleets sailed from here to the Americas. A papal edict gave Spain sole rights to trade with the colonies. As Spain's primary port, Sevilla ruled the New World.

NAT'L. TOURIST OFFICE OF SPAIN

C.

D.

NAT'L. TOURIST OFFICE OF SPAIN

ROE ANNE WHITE

A.

B.

NAT'L. TOURIST OFFICE OF SPAIN

C.

RICHARD CUCKSON

In contrast to the jetset atmosphere of Marbella and Majorca, Sevilla is representative of classical Spain. The city, with its magnificent Moorish architecture, drama, art, and mystery, was a muse to Beethoven, Mozart, Rossini, Verdi, Bizet, and Buñuel. The Golden Tower guards the river. In the old section of town there is a large and fabulous cathedral, in addition to the Alcazar (Moorish Palace) and several other grand museums and palaces of opulent design.

Sailing upriver offers a different view of Spanish cultural life. Some cruising yachts opt to winter in the sanctuary of Sevilla, and their owners have enjoyed festivals, flamenco, bullfights and sophisticated art. Sevilla's gilded and baroque architecture is a lively backdrop for celebrations, which are jubilant and unrestrained, as though the underlying passions of Catholicism have been temporarily unleashed.

A. Port of Javea
B. Torre del Oro, Sevilla
C. M/Y Trump Princess (Nabila) in Puerto Banus
D. Voyager in the Straits of Gibraltar
E. Gibraltar Harbor as seen from the Old Town

GIBRALTAR

The monumental headland of Gibraltar forms one end of the strategic portal to the Mediterranean, the legendary Pillars of Hercules. Past this point flow all the cargos and intrigues of the complex life contained within.

Control of the tiny port of Gibraltar, contiguous to the Spanish landmass, has always been a point of territorial contention, but for this century it lies in the hands of the British.

The specter of the Rock itself is astonishing, shot through with caves and tunnels that are actually inhabited by apes. The rainward side has been converted to a huge water catchment to quench the thirst of Gibraltar's growing population. Under this monolith, the swift waters and considerable traffic of the entire Mediterranean Sea converge, and in current and congestion try to pass through one small hole. The extraordinary currents produced by such a confluence offer terrific opposition to small-powered boats in anything but ideal conditions, so departure strategy is always a big topic among the skippers.

Known to cruising yachtsmen as an excellent port for repairs and provisioning, the Gibraltar yacht clubs, marinas and the old "destroyer pens," though perhaps not enchanting, have been the scene of some very useful refits and happy reunions. The pubs, which collect travelers in-bound and out, have become a veritable archive of informally-exchanged stories and information.

D.

JEANETTE PHILLIPPS

JEANETTE PHILLIPPS

E.

Cabo de Trafalgar lies astern and although the breeze is light, "Voyager" slides along effortlessly on placid waters. At last all traces of land have disappeared; the shoals and reef are behind us and the heaviness that always shrouds my chest, worrying over positions, current, and the plethora of ships plying the Straits, has given way to a sense of relief and freedom.

Our last three passages through the Straits of Gibraltar have been in gales with full working lowers, driving into force nine squalls trying desperately to separate the rig from hull. But for all my inadequacies, and those of her crew, Voyager has for over twenty-one years protected us and brought us to our destination safely.

Gibraltar becomes more interesting with each visit. The proprietors of the shops and restaurants are unusually friendly, and more than accommodating. At the "Old Vic," the owner sat with us eating "fish and chips," telling us of all the problems Gibraltarian merchants face. With the Spanish border closed, millions of tourist dollars remain on the Costa del Sol and even with low airfares, comparatively few make the trek from England.

The water catchment areas on the eastern side are lined with galvanized sheet metal – white-washed and not cement – as I had assumed when on the summit a year ago. Its longevity is questionable in this hostile salt air and it no longer has the capacity for a burgeoning population. In fact, the land area that can be utilized of its total two square miles – for housing, hotels and shops – is very little. The Rock occupies so much, and what remains is saturated and poorly planned. The old town appears to be built upon an older model and has a certain charm, having the scale of its medieval counterpart, although little remains except for fortifications. Most of the space is given to the military (Gibraltar's primary function), and probably is the reason that Spain, even with its exuberant new democracy, will not completely open the border. There is no space for crops and essentially no industry – importation without exportation. A rather frail dependency on the tiny mother island, itself of questionable strength.

Peter Phillipps

Peter Phillipps
From the log of S/Y *Voyager* • 29 May 1983 • Day One: Gibraltar to Tenerife .

PORTUGAL & BISCAY

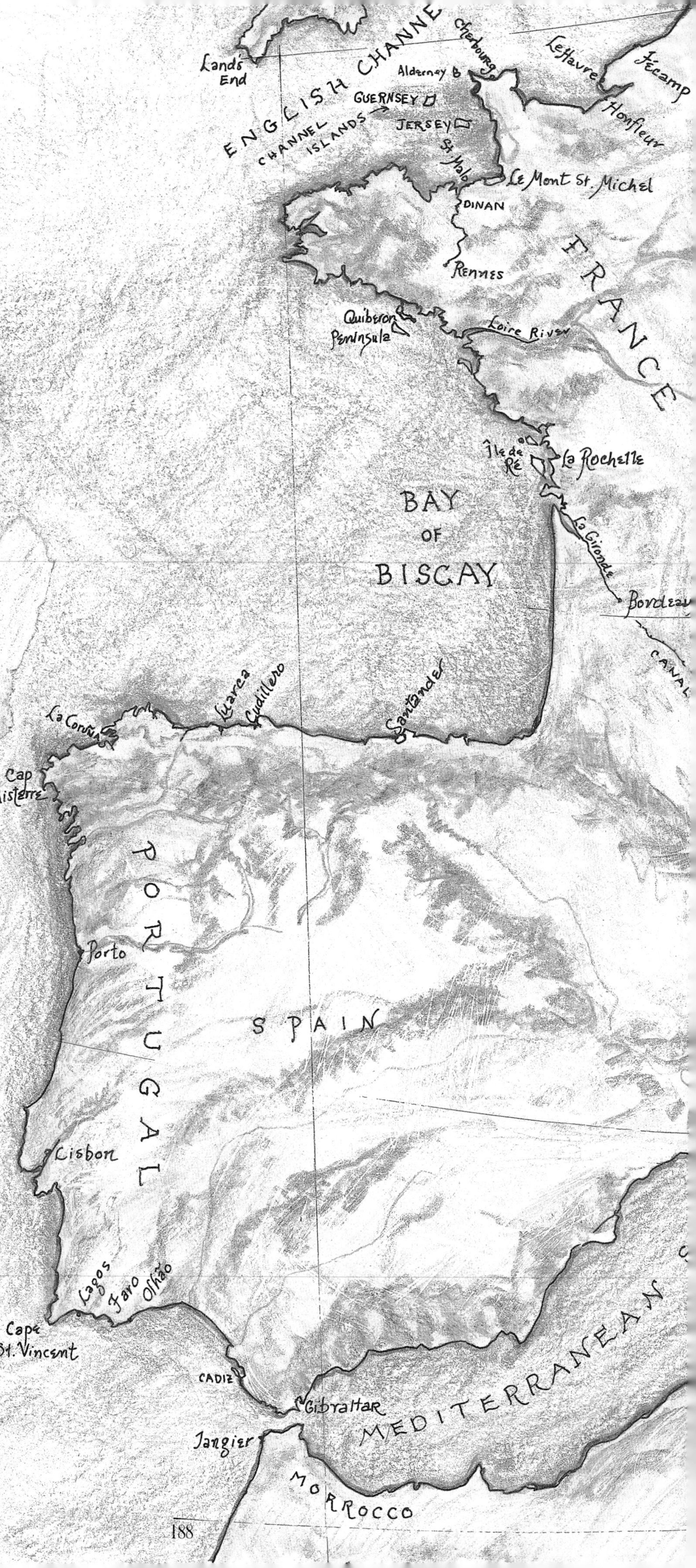

Land's End
ENGLISH CHANNE
Cherbourg
LeHavre
Fécamp
Honfleur
Alderney
GUERNSEY
JERSEY
CHANNEL ISLANDS
St. Malo
Le Mont St. Michel
DINAN
Rennes
FRANCE
Quiberon Peninsula
Loire River
Île de Ré
La Rochelle
La Gironde
Bordeau
CANAL
BAY OF BISCAY
La Coruña
Luarca
Cudillero
Santander
Cap Finisterre
PORTUGAL
Porto
SPAIN
Lisbon
Lagos
Faro
Olhão
Cape St. Vincent
CADIZ
Gibraltar
Tangier
MEDITERRANEAN
MORROCCO

30°
28°
26° W
38° N
FLORES
GRACIOSA
FAIAL
São Jorge
Terceira
Horta
Pico
S. Miguel
THE AZORES
Sta. Maria

ROE ANNE WHITE

PORTUGAL & BISCAY

Remote and rural, a sliver at the end of a continent, and further isolated by years of dictatorship, Portugal has developed a personality quite independent of its neighbor Spain and the rest of Europe. Portuguese fishermen may well have been the first to "discover" the Grand Banks of the New World. Portugese national history and monuments seem to have reached a dramatic head during the years of the Discoveries. Since that time, the Portuguese have been steadily enriching their culture, academically as well as economically.

The Algarve is a sunny region of cork and olive groves which has been discovered in the past decade by sailors and travelers. It is a region of subtle contours and gentle, hardworking people. Numerous ports are tucked into this indented coast: Lagos, Portimao, Faro and Olhao.

LINDA RUSSELL

A. B.

LINDA RUSSELL

The sailing was easy and pleasant, and the unspoiled river and countryside were beautiful, unlike the Guadalquivir, which ran through marshy lowlands and had been deepened and straightened in places, and had a somewhat artificial look. The Guadiana was natural and untouched and ran through gentle rolling hills. We passed small vineyards, fig and olive trees and fields of corn and melons. We saw farmers loading hay on patient donkeys and men rolling hogsheads and smaller casks of dark wood down to the river where they were washed and soaked. Sometimes we heard the tinkling of bells around the necks of goats and sheep. We continued upstream about 13 nautical miles until the tide turned and anchored at a hamlet called Foz do Odeleite. What could have been better, a perfectly sheltered anchorage and peace and quiet. The only sounds were from kingfishers, magpies, and orioles.

Hal Roth

Hal Roth
American writer/ photographer/ yachtsman

HAL ROTH

C.

D.

COMPLIMENTS OF HEYWARD ASSOCIATES

LISBON

The approach to Lisbon on the Tagus Estuary is majestic. This mighty river flows out of the hills with a vengeance, and the mouth can be boisterous when it meets opposing winds and tide. After braving the ravages of the Atlantic and the Bay of Biscay, it is not uncommon for sailors to think they will be secure here, only to find themselves in a roiling, confused sea. It is prudent to plan your entry to coincide with the inflowing tide. Lisbon is tremendously scenic, surrounded by rolling, fragrant green hillsides and the resorts of Estoril and Cascais. Not so long ago it was common to encounter *fahluas,* the traditional sailing cargo lighters, tacking around the river mouth with uncontainerized cargo.

Some miles upstream is the Belem Yacht Basin, framed by the handsomely engineered Salazar Suspension Bridge. Behind a legion of masts and rigging rises the renowned sculptural monument to Prince Henry the Navigator. It is trite to talk about sunsets being magnificent, but here on the Tagus River looking out to the Atlantic, they are truly special. If you are anxious to leave your boat behind, there is good train service into the entrancing city.

Lisbon is a city of contrasts, with dark hills hinting of secrets, and bright gardens, grace and music. A thousand pastel streets with tiled arches invite wandering. The Old Town that crowns the prominent hilltop has a depth of history. Varying degrees of poverty and oppression have refined the pathos in the Portuguese peasantry, and it is hauntingly expressed by the singers of *fado* (a mournful Portuguese song). It is not uncommon to hear the women wail out their sad music while hanging laundry or scrubbing their doorsteps.

A. Douro River, Portugal
B. The Algarve
C. Guadiana River
D. Salazar Suspension Bridge, Lisbon
page 187: San Estaban, Spain

PORTO

Cruising yachts can follow in the wake of the wine traders and sail into Porto. This town situated on the River Douro (river of gold) is famous for port wine. Historically, Porto was the center of a trade association which filled the coffers of several countries. The Romans initiated the trade, etching out the wine route that extends from the Roman Empire colonies of Portus and Cale on either side of the Douro River to England. The name Portugal is derived from Portus and Cale. Porto sired Henry the Navigator, and launched discoveries of the Far East and the New World. It still bustles with modern cargo: sans the panache of the colorful *fahluas*. Still, the Old Town retains the charm of bygone days. Casks and barrels, as in centuries past, are stacked up on the seafront, along with great piles of cork and salt fish. The yacht harbor is at Leixoes.

Soft green mountains and almost vertical fields partitioned with a grid of sugarcane surround us as we enter Horta, except for the seawall on the port side lined with workboats and yachts and the colorful signatures painted by visitors of years past.

There are visually exciting harbors everywhere in this world. Perhaps it is the location of this one that makes Horta so special; I crossed an ocean to get to this temporary refuge. Or perhaps what stays with me more is not just the way a sailor is physically received by the natives when he approaches from the sea, but the warmth exuded by these people. Horta is a home with more friends and family than one could dream of.

Everyone in the harbor has been to sea. They know all about you before you tie up. There is a common bond which breaks down the standard formalities when meeting new friends, and no time is wasted.

A group of our new friends gathered aboard for dinner since we had the largest cockpit. Everyone brought some part of the meal, including their own plates and utensils, making the clean-up no more a chore than usual. An Englishman played a small string instrument he was given in Polynesia, and as we sang along (sea chanties are universal); a small sloop pulled alongside with two crew exhausted from their long beat from England. They were greeted with food and drink and music, and we knew all about them already.

The natives of Horta really understand the sea, what it means to be out there, whether fishing or whaling, sailing a cargo from one island to another, or just cruising through. There are immaculate public baths and the Café Sport, where gin and tonics are 40 cents, beer 15 cents and money can be changed any day, any time; a mail drop, provisioning and laundry are all taken care of by Peter, the owner. And it is not unusual to be invited home to chat over a Maciera, despite the language barrier.

As we prepare to sail off, our clean clothes are spread over bushes on the hills to dry, bread is being baked twice to cut down the moisture content. We've been well taken care of; it's difficult to leave. But thanks to our friends, we are rested and ready to face the sea once again.

Jeanette Phillipps

Jeanette Phillipps
Architectural designer/ photographer/ yacht owner

THE AZORES

The Azores were uninhabited when they were found by Sherif Mohammed al Edrisi in the 12th century. His log noted the presence of many hawks. The Portuguese claimed the islands in 1444, and named them the *Acores* (hawks). This group of nine islands, conveniently located in Mid-Atlantic, became the way station for a plethora of seaborne enterprises. Pirates, whalers, and merchants brought their influence, and the fledgling community of Portuguese fishermen amalgamated the lot.

Some people firmly believe that the Azores are the surviving crowns of the lost continent Atlantis. These islands were born of some violent cataclysm. Their topography is a tapestry of contrasts; jagged rock upheavals and a barren moonscape intersect rolling terraced fields of fertile green. For a people tenuously clinging to a crag of rocks in the tempestuous mid-ocean, the Azorians belie any image of austerity or woebegone hardship. They are hardworking, but also fun-loving and exuberant people who seem to exult in the visits of passing ships.

The main harbor of Horta, on the island of Faial, is flanked by sheer bluffs. It shelters a lovely village, behind which the terraced fields and vineyards ascend rapidly up the steep slopes of Faial. Sailors from all over the world and from all manner of craft have left their artistic signatures on Horta's seawall, a fabulous mural of seafaring testimony which is almost filled now. A new seawall is under construction for the next generation of voyagers.

JEANETTE PHILLIPPS

A. B.

JAMES WALLEN

C.

JAMES WALLEN

A. Artistic signatures on Horta's sea wall, Faial
B. San Miguel, Azores
C. Punta del Gada
Painting by Peter Carr

ROE ANNE WHITE

A.

BAY OF BISCAY

Back on the mainland, we leave Portugal and proceed north into Spain again, where the land becomes wild and fjord-like. The shores of Galicia are indented with many magnificent rias; steep drowned glacial river valleys, which offer shelter and remarkable cruising in settled weather. Places like Villagarcia and Vigo give spectacular glimpses inland of a region unlike any other in Iberia.

Even though the river inlets are secure enough, the winds and waves off Cape Finisterre often dictate that a prudent mariner give the entire landmass a wide berth.

'Finis terre' — the name itself sounds menacing. Many vessels have 'finished' their careers off this Cape during the notorious storms of Biscay.

Many a pleasure sailor, after experiencing the tumultuous Bay of Biscay on a maiden voyage out from England, has found a safe haven on the colorful coast of Asturias in northern Spain. There are some wonderful unknown harbors tucked into these bluff highlands, a coastline reminiscent of Big Sur. Yachts are a rarity. Though the Asturians do not court tourism, they

San Esteban, a rather plain village full of colorful people, is a former thriving coal port, now decrepit. The only thing that remains of its once booming trade is the rusting, defunct loading chutes and railroad sidings. The local industry today is the breaking up of discarded ships. We watched worn out vessels arrive, get dismantled, and pulled out to sea. The yard was our favorite site for Sunday strolls, latent salvagers that we are — such a bounty of beautiful brass fittings, carved teak lockers, marble counters, and wooden ship furnishings , waiting to be burned or sold as scrap. We wished we had a huge boat to save these treasures, but we were destined for Greece, not to become merchants.

We had the engine work done in the neighboring fishing port of Cudillero. The feeling of this place is timeless. It is a teacup harbor, surrounded by steep hillsides, with just a narrow channel opening onto the Bay. Its charming village is perched on the seemingly vertical cliffs. The tiny harbor sheltered a fleet of fishing boats, often hauled up on the strand. The approach by land is dramatic. You drive through a remote and rugged landscape, halting on the brink of a precipice, overlooking red-tiled roofs.

We were the only foreigners there and our activities were the topic of friendly gossip. The locals were extremely helpful,took us into their homes, and led us on fascinating forays to the countryside. Caves filled with prehistoric paintings, and many historical buildings and shrines embellish a landscape that is quite grandly beautiful.

After Christmas, and its attendant Spanish pageantry, we finally set sail for the Mediterranean. We set out in mildly uncomfortable weather, but before nightfall the wind began to howl and, reluctantly, we put into the safety of Luarca. There we found many fishing boats from up and down that stretch of coast, who had put in to wait out a storm which promised to be a good one. Day after day they stayed in port and advised us to do the same. The storm raged on, and the lively young lads and oldtimers, sitting on net heaps, yarned all day, and interrogated us as to our mission. We explained our intention of sailing around the Mediterranean, and eventually home across the Atlantic, the Caribbean, through Panama to California. The fishermen were disbelieving and dumbstruck. They looked at our pretty little Foye, and sadly shook their heads. We would surely meet a watery death. They would never see the prints of these pictures they were so happy to smile for. We wouldn't even make Gibraltar. Fortunately they were mistaken, and I did send the pictures along. We never heard again from the fishermen of Luarca, but I keep a happy memory still of the friendships we developed on the majestic coast of Asturias.

Roe Anne White

Roe Anne White
Photographer/ Owner of S/Y *Foye*

love visitors, and treat them royally.

Across the Biscay Bay into France is the river Gironde, the northern terminus of the *Canal du Midi*. This lovely stretch of water was conceived and constructed by Louis XIV to enhance trade in this corner of France. The canal makes a scenic and fascinating short route to the Mediterranean for boats of shallow draft.

In Roman times, the island of Oleron (then called *Ularius*) occupied a strategic point at the mouth of the Gironde Estuary between Bordeaux and La Rochelle. The Charente Maritime island group does not command the strategic importance it once did, but the islands provide a delightful haven for cruising. The islands of Noirmoutier and Oleron are already moored by bridge to the mainland, but L'Île de Ré, off the coast of La Rochelle, remains the preserve of sailors and fishermen. Saint Martin de Ré is a charming port with a central island linked by a footbridge. Around the other side, L'Hebaudière is a lively port, popular with yachtsmen who come to consume the sardines and lobster which have made it famous. A simple, salty pleasure.

The Vieux Port of La Rochelle is guarded by a picturesque trio of towers, originally built to protect it from marauding armadas. La Rochelle and L'Île de Ré survived the hard times and became prosperous in both the fur and wine trade, and enjoyed a certain autonomy in New World commerce.

The harbor is festooned with great rafts of fishing boats that provide the wharfside restaurants with aromatic seafood bouquets. The boats are there awaiting the tide, their nets and mooring flags waving against a lively background of spires, tiled roofs and domes. Arcaded streets lead up from the port through graceful shopping and residential districts, where the houses reflect the architectural splendor of centuries past. The foot-weary sailor can make use of community bicycles to further savor the delights, treasures and parks of this socialist town.

ROE ANNE WHITE

B. C.

ROE ANNE WHITE

D.

COMPLIMENTS OF HEYWARD ASSOCIATES

A. Tiny port of Cudillero, Spain
B. San Esteban, Spain
C. Fishermen of Asturias
D. Fahlua in Porto

BRITTANY

North of the Loire Estuary by way of Nantes or the Côte d'Amour, boats of shallow draft may continue inland through a fascinating canal system that bisects Brittany. A journey best made by barge or houseboat, this route enables sailors to glimpse the fortresses, farmland and people of this varied region. The Manche-Atlantic Canal takes a scenic climb of 47 locks up and over the Breton hills and ends at St. Malo.

At the Quiberon Peninsula, there is a welcome relief from "Biscay nerves." Leave your boat in the quiet port while you relax and take the waters at the spa for thalassotherapy. Seaweed, saltwater baths and ionized salt air restore well-being.

Just inland from Quiberon is the beautiful Gulf of Morbihan. The Morbihan region is noted for an abundance of megalithic monuments dating back to prehistoric times. The island of Er Lannic in the gulf has a famous group of *menhirs* (prehistoric monuments).

NATALIE GUILLAUME

A.

B.

SOREN RASMUSSEN

The port of La Trinité offers access to this gulf and some of the best sailing areas in Brittany. The islands of Belle-Île, Île aux Moines, Houat, Hoedic and Groix are each unique and delightful destinations. Oyster producers dwell on the shores of the gulf. Oysters from the gulf combined with the scallops from Quiberon and the fresh produce of the coastal plain comprise a mouth-watering moveable feast.

La Trinité sponsors a multi-hull race at the end of March, and a regatta for traditionally-rigged vessels in mid-August. Boats come from Brittany, Normandy, England and Ireland to participate. A number of Breton navigators, having sailed the seas of the world, have retired here.

Brittany has long been recognized as the lonely, beautiful province of France which supplied the mother country with mariners and filled the larder with seafood. Breton sailors peopled the French Navy, and Breton emigrants carried their culture and seafaring lore to far shores around the world. With its prow jutting into the Atlantic, this land of *Armorica* (the Breton name) is blessed with a huge selection of harbors. The seashore pleasures of entertainment, sport, health spas and superb cuisine have been discovered, and resort and marina facilities are quite abundant.

Concarneau is a huge fishing port with yachting facilities available. The original town is an island fortress which has outgrown its medieval walls, and is now connected to land by a bridge of solid stone.

Rounding Cape Finisterre, you are in for a remarkable stretch of coast and delightful villages, from Aber W'rach in the Baie des Anges to the Côte d'Emeraude. This route winds past beaches of sugar-white sand, huge rocky headlands and expansive tidal marsh. The channel tides wash beaches and towns that were either instrumental in or laid to waste by artillery on the infamous D-Day.

A. La Trinité, France
B. Port of Quiberon
C. Towers at harbor entrance, La Rochelle
D. Streets of Honfleur

FERENC MATE

C.

D.

FRENCH GOV'T. TOURIST OFFICE

UNITED KINGDOM

DANA JINKINS

UNITED KINGDOM

Four hundred years ago the island of Britain underwent a transformation from sheepfarming to sea power that could be likened to Japan's emergence this century. Merchant traders became skilled seamen who brought great wealth to the south coast of England. A maritime power encompassed many things — bravery, finesse and enterprise, as well as acts of piracy, slave-trading and treachery — all in the name of God and England.

As time elapsed, the English Channel became an important thoroughfare totally disproportionate to its size.

The strategic importance of this channel has been illustrated in many battles. The Channel also presents a formidable symbolic frontier, separating the British from the Continentals, whom they flout, envy, ridicule, compete with, yet romanticize, and love to mingle with when they are on holiday. The allegorical gulf is strewn on both shores with interesting historical testimony affirming this ambivalence.

Years of maritime power on this island of islands spawned a hearty breed of sailors, and developed a coastline of wonderful ports. England has probably contributed more than any other nation to the tradition of pleasure sailing.

Pin Mill is a tiny hamlet on the banks of the tidal section of the River Orwell, on the East Coast of England. It lies about four miles upstream from the mouth of the river which is dominated by the ferry port of Harwich and the vast container port of Felixstowe.

Venture ashore and revitalize yourself with a pint of real ale at the "Butt and Oyster" pub. In the 17th century, this pub was believed to have been a smugglers' haven. Today, during the summer, it is an increasingly popular tourist watering hole; when winter comes it reverts to a dive for the locals — a few fishermen, the odd die-hard sailor, and the bargees.

For the past 100 years or so, Pin Mill was a popular laying-up spot for the colorful Thames barges. Tradition continues, if in a slightly modified form. Many of the old barges lie up along the shoreline, in varying degrees of decay; some have been converted to houseboats and vie for space along the wooded bank with old lighters and Dutch barges.

On the first weekend of July each year the Pin Mill Sailing Club hosts the annual Barge Match. The Match was initiated in the 1960s with fewer than a dozen competitors; today there are over 50 barges in the race, indicative of the renewed enthusiasm of both individuals and companies in maintaining this aspect of Britain's maritime heritage.

Patricia Dent

Patricia Dent
British Journalist/ Photographer

PATRICIA DENT

A.

B.

PATRICIA DENT

EAST ANGLIA

The River Thames estuary has silted ever farther out to sea, through a maze of channels among featureless marsh and lowlands. In the upper reaches, there are many delightful ports such as Pin Mill and Maldon. These harbors are noteworthy for their fleets of old Thames barges which were once used to handle all the London cargo trade.

ISLE OF WIGHT

This massive block of limestone protects the Solent and the mainland port of Southhampton. Cowes, on the Isle of Wight, is the terminus of many regattas and long distance races, so the horizon is cheery with colorful sails.

The tides here are nothing to trifle with. When you see a name like Portland Race on the chart, it means the tides *can* race there, and you should stay in port until the moon favors the direction in which you hope to be going.

LYME REGIS

Lyme Bay between Portland and Brixham is the scene of a gradual transition from Anglo-Saxon, London-rule mentality to the Celtic pride of Dorset, Devon and Cornwall. Dickensian dramas and characters from Hardy have already furnished our imaginations with strong images of this coast. Tor Bay, where Napoleon was held captive, has not known such fame since, and the former port of Lyme Regis has eroded in a cascade of fossils and chalky cliff.

This port harbors more history and literary worth than ships these days. The fashionable Georgian waterfront and its curving breakwater, the Cobb (originally built around 1300), were the setting for Jane Austen's novel *Persuasion* and John Fowles's *The French Lieutenant's Woman.*

A. Butt and Oyster Pub, Pin Mill
B. Thames Barge Race
C. Maldon as seen through the rigging
D. Cowes, Isle of Wight
E. The Cobb, Lyme Regis

ROE ANNE WHITE

C. D.

ROE ANNE WHITE

E.

ROE ANNE WHITE

ROE ANNE WHITE

A.

RIVER DART

After a long sail across Lyme Bay, the River Dart provides a welcome port of call. The entrance is fairly narrow, but plenty deep. Kingswear Castle and Dartmouth Castle guard the entrance. The latter dates from 1481. Locals love to tell the story of how a 750-foot chain resting on six barges was transported across the harbor to the opposite shore to protect the port from raiders.

PLYMOUTH

Plymouth Sound is one of the Channel's perfect natural harbors and the gateway to Devonshire. Approach to the sound is flanked by the moors of Cornwall and the Devon coastline. Captains Drake, Bligh, Scott and Chichester sailed forth from this port. The Mayflower embarked from Plymouth. The Mayflower pier and its barbican, or watergate, now provide pleasant berthing alongside the historic Elizabethan quarter. The harbor is always astir with sailboats, ferries and naval and merchant ships.

When visiting Dartmouth, if time allows, take a trip up the River Dart to the old Anglo-Saxon hill fort (now the town) of Totnes. It's a delightful 10 or so miles, meandering through bucolic Devon. Be sure to get an up-to-date chart as the going can get very thin at low water, but with a rising half-tide or better, it is fairly simple. Some good-sized freighters bringing lumber from Norway make the trip all the way to the docks at Totnes.

Very little has changed, and there is no new development to mar the scenery — lush rolling meadows and mature English woods that come right down to the water's edge, grazing cows, and farms and coppices scattered about the hillsides. The small village of Dittisham about halfway upstream hides in a little valley. A couple of creeks are home to old-time ramshackled boatyards that have seen better days, but they make a peaceful stop for anyone wanting to escape the hustle of a marina. Several large and imposing mansions overlook the river, purportedly built by privateers with their ill-gotten booty, and occasionally you see an old stone boathouse nestled by the waters's edge.

A pleasant respite for the ocean sailor, a quiet interlude away from the open sea, and an admirable way to reflect on something other than 360 degrees of water and horizon.

David & Avril Howe

David and Avril Howe
Professional Yacht Captain and Chef

A. Waterfront, Dartmouth
B. Daphne du Maurier's house, Fowey
C. A view of Fowey from Polruan

FOWEY

The quiet port of Fowey (rhymes with Troy) once ruled the western Channel. The piratical "gallants" of Fowey terrorized Channel shipping as far back as the Crusades, and a hope of immunity encouraged other vessels to take on Fowey crew. Legitimate trade then grew in wine, pilgrims, wool and metals. Profiting by the knowledge and connections of the pirates' sons, Fowey became prominent. Like the entrance to the River Dart, Fowey also had a chain, used as protection against foes of all sorts, that stretched across the harbor mouth over to Polruan,

The famous Stephens' merchant fleet of schooners from Fowey sailed into the 1920s on extremely fast hulls, carrying cargo across oceans in record time. They all had "Little" in their names, like *Little Mystery* and *Little Pet.* Some of the fleet succumbed to the U-Boats in World War I, but they continued trading into the 1930s. They are fondly remembered by yachting visitors and the denizens of this traditional, quaint harbor.

Twenty-four miles east of my home port of Falmouth lies the town of Fowey with its picturesque harbour sheltered between the village of Polruan and the town itself. Though a busy port, with many clay barges plying their trade between Cornwall and the Continent, it has lost none of its Cornish charm.

Once a year the Fowey Regátta is held where the locals mix with visiting yachts, including the famous Falmouth Gaff-Rigged Oyster Boats. The climax of the Regatta Week's frivolities and racing happens when the oyster boats, or working boats as they are known locally, race each other within the confines of the inner harbour. Ribald challenges issue forth from competing crews, and because the first prize is a cup and the second prize a barrel of beer, the race for second place is intense.

After the race has ended and crews and spectators have come ashore, the night air is filled with the sound of Cornish voices singing their hearts out. The whole harbour seems to capture the warmth of its friendly inhabitants. It is always sad to sail away from such an enchanting haven, but at least there is next year to look forward to.

Robin Taylor
Skipper/ Working Boat *Endeavour* - Built 1903

DANA JINKINS

B. C.

DANA JINKINS

DANA JINKINS

A. B.

MEVAGISSEY

What with the proximity of France and the exorbitant Anglo-Saxon taxes, smuggling was a natural offspring of the merchant trade. The west country and the proud Cornish people felt no greater loyalty to England than to Brittany. Mevagissey was once a smugglers' notch. Also, in the 18th and 19th centuries, one of the largest centers for pilchard fisheries (herring-like fish) was operating there. Today it is still a working fishing town, but because of its inherent charm, it is also a thriving tourist center in the summer. Winding narrow streets with pastel cottages lead to "fish and chips" concessions, "Cornish pasties," and confections. Most of the moorings in the outer harbor belong to fishermen, but if you can find a space, the surroundings are extremely colorful.

DANA JINKINS

FALMOUTH

The approach to Falmouth and the River Fal is guarded by two Tudor castles. Following an auspicious start in the Biscay pirate business, the mariners of Falmouth undertook the more respectable trade of couriers to the colonies. When Falmouth's packets were replaced by steam, the large and well-protected harbor remained a communications center for overseas trade. Intercontinental skippers reported to "Falmouth for orders" to receive telegraph messages from their owners indicating whether or not to regroup, reprovision or wait for wind.

Once inside the fortress gates, the river opens up to a magnificent network of tributaries. The main harbor at Falmouth shelters a substantial commmercial fleet and occasional ships from Her Majesty's Royal Navy. The working boats indigenous to the River Fal are gaff-rigged oyster boats generally about 28 feet with amazingly long bowsprits. Summer evenings, the river is replete with yachts of every class enjoying competition in a regularly scheduled race, or just enjoying a sunset cruise.

The village of St. Mawes, across the River Fal, has a lovely anchorage away from the bustle of Falmouth. The wandering creeks of the estuary provide many quiet refuges for yachtsmen. Marsh, forest and changing river channels have limited development, making for wonderful secluded cruising.

The Helford River is another spectacularly beautiful waterway, less developed than Falmouth. It was the inspiration for Daphne du Maurier's novel, *Frenchman's Creek*. The river has large oyster beds that purportedly date back to Roman times. These beds have discouraged the spreading of moorings and other commercial development.

DANA JINKINS

C.

D.

DANA JINKINS

A. Aerial view of Mevagissey
B. Mevagissey's idyllic inner harbor
C. A pastoral anchorage up the River Fal
D. Figurehead, Falmouth

DANA JINKINS

A.

B.

DANA JINKINS

THE LIZARD AND LAND'S END

The curling, indented coast of South Cornwall comes to a dramatic granite conclusion at Land's End and the Lizard. This region of reefs and pinnacles with tremendous waves from the fetch of the whole Atlantic has been a menace to sailors for centuries. The Lizard deserves its reputation as the maker of shipwrecks and widows.

The hearty fisherfolk of these Cornish villages have responded heroically to the rescue of marooned sailors and ships in distress. There are many stories of the valiant lifeboatmen of Cadgwith and Mousehole. When the fury of the storm had her way, however, the Cornishmen supplemented their meager incomes by salvaging the misfortunes of others. The fish and the flotsam and the wrecks were just considered part of the bounty of the sea.

Cadgwith, north of the Lizard, is a working fishing port, a picturesque village where the boats are pulled up daily onto the beach with a big old windlass. The harbor is not protected, but it is enchanting.

St. Michael's Mount is a miniature reflection of Mont Saint-Michel, whose monks founded a monastery here in the 11th century. (It was part of the package tour for pious travelers in the Middle Ages.) Ancient Greek voyagers described coming to this mount in 300 B.C. for Cornish tin. Scribes, unused to tides in the Mediterranean, eagerly reported this phenomenon that made an island out of a peninsula and enabled the tin gatherers to roll their wagons out at ebb tide. Both this harbor and its neighbor at Mousehole are only accessible from half-tide on.

DANA JINKINS

C.

DANA JINKINS

D.

E.

DANA JINKINS

A. Falmouth Harbor
B. Evening Regatta, Falmouth
C. Fisherman of Cadgwith
D. Low tide, St. Michael's Mount
E. Mousehole on a Sunday afternoon

JOHN DONOVAN

A. B.

JAMES WALLEN

My memories of Dingle center on the scene as we first cruised into the bay. I think this was the first land that Lindbergh saw when he finished his crossing. As we neared the dock, all kinds of people emerged, obviously curious to see this old boat full of "hippies" coming in. We made quite a contrast to all these guys in their tweed coats and hats. I remember the silence when we threw the docklines. It couldn't have lasted 30 seconds before all kinds of people were hollering welcomes, wondering what corner of the far ocean we hailed from. Soon a giant local salmon was heaved aboard, and a bottle of hootch for our channel guide. For the next week we enjoyed celebrity status in town. One day I was walking along and a nun stopped me in the street and asked me if I was from the boat on the jetty. When I said I was, she welcomed me to Ireland, and said that she was sure I'd have a good time in Dingle as there were 52 pubs. We checked out quite a few, heard some great Irish music and were introduced to the glorious pints of Guinness that became a nightly ritual. I can still see the rings of foam on me glass.

Mark

Mark Padbury
Master Shipwright/ sailor

IRELAND

Ireland is an ancient land which has preserved a great deal of its tradition from prehistory and medieval times. One senses this immediately. The perimeter of the rugged and mountainous coastline gives way to an extremely moist and green interior of rolling fields, forest and bogs. The plentitude of rainfall makes for a high level of water vapor in the air. Perhaps this accounts for the misty dreamlike quality of the landscape. Also, the rain must have something to do with all that green! They say that a true Irishman can distinguish 40 shades of green; in any event, 'greenness' seems to be the superlative quality reported to us by visiting sailors, followed by friendliness and Guinness.

WEST COAST

The west country, the stronghold of Gaelic speech, is littered with ruins and antiquities. The name Dingle was derived from *Daingean*, the Irish word for fortress. This spectacular peninsula unfolds under the "holy mountain" of Cnocknadobar through misty verdure to a wild and rock-bound head where it meets the Atlantic Ocean.

Dingle Bay was the landfall for a crew of friends on a Baltic trader, the *Lene Marie*, after crossing the Atlantic. Understandably, the lure of *terra firma* would look good to anyone after 30 days at sea, but this vibrant green tapestry — unmistakably Ireland — was well appreciated by these valiant wanderers.

ISLE OF MAN

The inscription "The Isle of Man" on the stern of a vessel signifying her homeport has always intrigued me. Was it where Man originated? Or merely the Manx cats. The Manx culture is ancient, yet there is stone testimony to earlier inhabitants. Manxmen speak a different Gaelic, and are altogether quite peculiar. In any event, the Port of St. Mary's offers excellent shelter and a popular mustering spot for sailors.

DICK JOHNSON

C.

D.

DICK JOHNSON

If you like anchorages with atmosphere, what better than the ruins of a medieval castle on one point, and on the other, the remains of a manor house that was torched during the 'troubles' of the 20s, and the wreck of a fishing boat at the end of a stone-walled lagoon, with rhododendron and gorse bushes everywhere and water so clear that you can see your anchor 20 feet below.

That's Dunboy Harbor that leads off the west side of Piper Sound off Bantry Bay in Ireland, round the western side of Bere Island, on the way to the bustling fishing port of Castletownberehaven.

Local lore has it that the big house, owned by an Englishman, was selected to be fired and everyone was aware of the fact. When 'the lads' arrived at the front door they found it locked and barred against them. They axed down the door only to find the magnificent figure of the English butler standing in the hall. "His Lordship is not at home," was the greeting. The lads ignored him, pushing past to set light to everything they could find. As timbers started to fall and the torch party retreated, the butler, holding the door for the departing gang, is reputed to have said, "And whom shall I say called?"

The house itself is interesting, the way it is built around the base of an ancient tower in every conceivable architectural style, and on a multitude of levels. It was a folly of one of the Coates family, they of thread fame, and was never completed.

Dunboy is probably the most perfect setting that I have ever anchored in. It might have been the excellent weather we enjoyed, but I feel that it was more the amazing atmosphere of the place.

Dick Johnson
Editor of "Yachting World"

A. Kinsale, Ireland
B. Dingle Peninsula
C. Majestic Anchorage at Dunboy Harbor
D. Dunboy, Bantry Bay

HOLLAND

As children, we learned to associate Holland with tulips, windmills, cocoa, and the boy who put his finger in the dike. A large portion of the Netherlands was indeed underwater until dikes, canals and watermills reversed the tide. The new lowlands provided more living and working space and created perfect soil conditions for growing bulbs.

It is gratifying to sail into the heart of this waterbound land to the beautiful, bustling port city of Amsterdam. This city of canals — the Venice of the north — is a visual treat. The famous Dutch canal barges, some swank and some funky, line the canals. These floating domiciles are unique to Amsterdam. It's hard to say whether there are more barges or more bridges in Amsterdam. Sailors wanting to brave the canals must learn to do so without their masts.

Amsterdam owes its existence as a port to a fluke of nature that occurred in the 12th century. The North Sea inundated Holland and created an enormous body of water. The Dutch have since learned how to profit from their windfall coastline by developing a system of dikes to create more land.

Amsterdam represents an eclectic blend of styles, no doubt picked up from extensive trading ventures. Indonesian restaurants proliferate, wafting exotic aromas. The impression that lingers longest is the night view of this city whose decorative townhouses are reflected in canal after canal. If you are not exploring the city by boat, get that folding bicycle out from under your sailboard and use it! Everyone uses bicycles for transportation in this magical city.

The enduring presence of the sea has produced an excellent corps of hydro-engineers and boatbuilders. The term "Dutch boatbuilder" connotes excellence to mariners world-wide. A prodigious number of boatyards are ensconced around the canals. The craft of wooden boatbuilding has diminished in favor of aluminum and steel. The Federation of Dutch Shipbuilders once had seven members; now the two com-

DANA JINKINS

A.

B.

MATTHY DE WIJS

panies that call themselves "Feadship" are the Van Lent Yard and the De Vries Yard, known for their magnificent custom motoryachts. There are many more yards in this tiny country with fine reputations: Jongert, Amels, Diana, Diaship. Some yards, such as The Royal Huisman Shipyard in Vollenhove, are tucked away in cow fields. The Huisman Shipyard is a family-run business. Recently they rebuilt the old J-Boat *Endeavor*, but their primary business is producing incredibly high-tech high-quality megasailboats.

A sea trial for one of Huisman's latest engineering feats took place out of the tiny northern fishing village of Urk. The juxtaposition of a super modern Ron Holland-designed sailboat sitting in the harbor of a village that dates back to the Middle Ages was quite a remarkable sight. Some of the men from Urk still wear traditional fishermen's clothes with head coverings called *karpoets*, and the women wear *kraplap*, or gay blouses. A fishing museum in Urk exhibits interesting boats such as the ice-flat, a big wooden rowing boat with gliding runners underneath it.

Another quaint Dutch harbor is Enkhuizen, directly opposite Urk across the Ijsselmeer and north of Amsterdam. This historic port town dating from the 11th century is the home of traditional sailing craft and the Zuiderzee Museum, another boat Hall of Fame. The harbor is dominated by a monumental defense tower, the *Drommedaris*, built by the Dutch East and West India Company when Enkhuizen was in its heyday. Rising from the flats of Holland, it looks forbidding. The canaled city is protected from the sea by two extensive walls, the *Zeemuur* and the *Vestingwal*, which serve as good bike trails, as well as offering an elevated place for harbor-viewing.

Urk is a small famous old fishing village about 25 kilometers from our yard in Vollenhove. In the olden days it used to be at the "Zuiderzee," a saltwater sea connected to the North Sea. After they put the "Afsluitdijk" in (up north), it became a fresh-water lake, the "Ijsselmeer." The main business of Urk is fishing: the big coasters go to the North Sea for their catch. Urk is a very religious town and a lot of the older people still wear traditional clothes.

We usually take the yachts we build (with drafts under four meters) to Urk for finishing touches and sea trials. The people of Urk are very helpful to us, especially the harbourmaster. He tries to dock our boats in front of his house so he can keep a close eye on them. We have never been charged one penny for harbour fees.

We enjoy taking our clients touring around the countryside. We always take them to Urk for some fish (salted herring or sole). Many leave with wooden models of old fishing ships. There is an old man in Urk who makes the most beautiful models.

If we go for sea trials on the Ijsselmeer, we also like to go to Enkhuizen. If the draft of the vessel permits it, we try to get into the old harbour where all the old sailing barges are. Even though it's extremely crowded mid-summer, it is quite picturesque and there are wonderful restaurants. Both Enkhuizen and Muiden have Royal Yacht Clubs. Some of the members are our clients.

Wolter Huisman and Alice Huisman
Royal Huisman Shipyard
Vollenhove, Holland

DANA JINKINS

C.

D.

ANDERS HOEGH POST

Page 215: Fjallbacka, Sweden
A. Reflections in the canal
B. The distinctive architecture of Enkhuizen
C. Urk, Holland
D. The Frisian Islands

BAD NYT

A. B.

ALAIN GUILLOU

C.

ALAIN GUILLOU

GERMANY

The Frisian Islands in the North Sea are not strikingly beautiful, nor warm, nor historically enduring. The North Sea is claiming great pieces of them in winter storms and its shifting sands bewilder sailors who don't have the most up-to-date charts. The Frisian Islands' anchorages are enchanting in the bewitching sense of the word — no palm trees, no beaches, nothing to speak of but shifting sandbars. There is mystery here, as illustrated in *The Riddle of the Sands*, a novel of sea-borne intrigue by Erskine Childers. The ionized invigorating air here, reputed to be therapeutic — even aphrodisical — is referred to as *reizklima* (a stimulating climate).

Kiel, Germany commands the northern end of the Kiel Canal, the marine short cut across Denmark to the Baltic. This port gained its international yacht-racing acclaim 100 years ago under Kaiser Wilhelm II, who was a fanatic sailor. He created the *Kieler Woche* (Kiel Week), a race event to compete with Cowes Week, which it has now eclipsed.

Most of old Kiel was destroyed during World War II. The brick reconstruction along the waterfront, though not beautiful, is enlightened by much greenery and *Jugendstil* architectural motifs. The race week is accompanied by the *Spiellinie*, a carnival and crafts fair which lines Kiel's harborfront promenade.

SCANDINAVIA

Some people think of Scandinavia as one place; however, the individual countries that comprise this northern region of Europe — Norway, Denmark, Sweden, Finland and Iceland — are fiercely independent and proud of their national identity. Wherever you are in Scandinavia, the sea is never far off. This bond with the sea is the unifying force.

Viking sailors like a challenge. Because their cruising season is short and their grounds are vast, they take full advantage of propitious sailing conditions. Midnight sun shines on their capers, making for delightfully long daylight hours during the summer. Still, even in winter the Scandinavians are undaunted by cold and stormy weather. It makes the harbors more cozy and welcome in their opinion.

A. Flensburg, Germany
B. Kiel Week
C. Kiel Harbor during International Sailing Week
D. E. F. Sogndalsstranden, Norway

MIKE BEAL

D. E.

MIKE BEAL

F.

MIKE BEAL

We crossed from the Shetland Islands to Bergen, Norway, in our 33-foot sloop "Mitty" for a month of cruising in Norwegian waters. The sun set as we dropped anchor and rose as we dug it in. No darkness up here in late June. We're at latitude 60. Our friends, Ivor and Josephine Baker, joined us in Bergen where we bought loads of fresh salmon and sailed south to the Hardanger Fjord. This is the fjord that inspired the composer Grieg, and understandably so. Snow-covered mountains rise up on either side to 4000 feet. It is humbling, massive, silent. Too beautiful for words, only a symphony can do it justice.

We stopped for the night in Sundal, halfway up the fjord, to view the Bondhus Glacier. This was our favorite Norwegian harbor. We followed an irresistable urge to trek two miles straight up to be nearer to the glacier. The variety of blues was stunning. Ice blue is not just one shade. We were plagued by a mountain goat which was bent on licking all the salt off us, a task almost as monumental as our climb. Later that night we were invited home by a Norwegian army captain who dispelled an earlier opinion that the Norwegians are not hospitable.

Mike • Mitty Beal

Mike & Mitty Beal
Yacht Owners

A.

MIKE BEAL

NORWAY

The exceedingly long coast of Norway has breathtaking scenery in cruising grounds more temperate than one might expect in view of its close proximity to the Arctic Circle. The word fjord is almost synonomous with Norway, and there are indeed numerous fjords in this rugged country. The Oslo Fjord is deep and wide, with idyllic anchorages and villages set between rocky islets and pine-robed inlets.

Around on the west coast of Norway, the Hardanger and Sogne Fjords are some of the most spectacular. From seaward the coast appears rugged and barren, but as you sail into the fjords, the slopes become more radical and the intermittent fields more verdant.

Springtime blossoms add luster to the grandeur in Sogne Fjord, which divides into four fingers. Orchards thrive in the greenhouse effect created by the sun-warmed rock slopes and the moisture of the fjord. The rare combination of blossoming fruit trees on one side of the narrow fjord and the towering snow-capped mountains on the other is an unforgettable sight. The glaciers at the head of the fjord look like huge waterfalls.

Bergen is a large and prosperous, proud and beautiful city on the westernmost point of Norway. Bergen's signal peak, the Flöyen, rises abruptly to 1000 feet and offers an expansive view that sweeps from the curving shoreline to a semi-circle of mountains down to the fjord and out to the ocean. A funicular takes you to the top.

The harbor of Vågen in Bergen is surrounded by the old city, founded in the 11th century, and Nordnes Park that has a fortress. From the Flöyen, a pleasing pattern of wharves and warehouses, tidy cottages, narrow lanes, green parks and broad avenues greets the eye. The narrow warehouses on the quay survive from Hanseatic times and are still in service. They lend a handsome backdrop to the age-old fish market on the quay.

Ålesund (Eel Sound) is a beautiful and dynamic town on the coast north of Bergen. A repository of *Art Nouveau* architecture graces the many waterfingers of this calm harbor in the sound, as well as the road leading up to the Acropolis. A restaurant and a stadium at the top offer a magnificent view of town, fjords, mountains and the Norwegian Sea.

Trondheim was the original Viking harbor and the medieval capital of Norway. Founded in the 10th century, it sits on a triangle of land in a fjord. Many eras and many vessels have issued forth from this natural splendor. Vikings sailed their longboats to America and the countries comprising the Byzantine Empire.

Above Trondheim is a land of splendid isolation. The variety of stunning landscapes continues, but habitation becomes more scarce. There are farms and tiny fishing villages amid the glaciers at 62 degrees north. Small fleets of trawlers lying off these fjordic hamlets are a common sight. Their captains know all about going to sea in small ships and always welcome the intrepid voyageur.

SOREN RASMUSSEN

B.

C.

ROTEN BRAUN

A. Bondus Glacier, Sundale
B. Winter in Bergen
C. Famous fish market, Bergen
D. Aalesund, Norway

D.

SOREN RASMUSSEN

DENMARK

Denmark embraces land and water in the heart of Scandinavia. Copenhagen was for a long time the capital of Scandinavia, and in terms of personality and popularity, it still is. Not restricted by the more repressive laws of its neighbors, it is a capital of fun. Tivoli Gardens is a fanciful and beautifully landscaped amusement park right in the middle of the city. Danes enjoy the high seas and the islands belonging to their domain. From Langelinie, the statue of Hans Christian Anderson's "Little Mermaid" beckons. This little statue which has come to represent Copenhagen Harbor has had a dubious history—she has had her head chopped off more than once. The harbor is backed by gardens, a citadel, and The Royal Danish Yacht Club.

Copenhagen was founded upon its most strategic waterway, the sound between the North Sea and the Baltic Sea. A 12th century cleric-warrior fortified the small central island of Slotsholmen, which marked the genesis of this city. Copenhagen (købmands havn) means merchant's harbor.

One of my favorite harbours in Denmark is Dragor situated approximately 20 kilometers south of Copenhagen, not far from the Copenhagen International Airport. The harbour is a picturesque fishing-hamlet from the 17th century. It combines the old architecture with new facilities in a harmonious way. From there, you can visit museums and other sights. There is also ferry service to Sweden.

Valdemar Bandolowski
Director/ Danish America's Cup Challenge

ANDERS HOEGH POST

A. B.

JAMES WALLEN

The gracious old city is laced with canals. The Nyhavn Canal has become a gathering spot for all manner of classic and traditional vessels. Their rigging adds an interesting dimension to the architectural lines drawn by the 18th century houses that line the canal. Once this area was the domain of salty fishermen, tattoo parlors, and roughneck bars; today Nyhavn is replete with boutiques and cafés, but not to the detriment of its intrinsic charm.

Kronborg Castle (of Hamlet fame) guards the harbor at Elsinore and is a major attraction here at the doorway to Sweden. The castle was built in the 15th century to maintain Danish sovreignty and fill her coffers. Every vessel that passed through this strategic gate to Northern Europe had to pay dues. Buildings were erected with these monies which form the core of the city today. Elsinore is a favorite yachting center for races, and embarkations to the Danish Riviera are made from here.

Pleasure sailors passing through Scandinavia have the venerable fishing trade to thank for the many havens available to them after having experienced the rigors of a North Sea passage. The fishing industry can also be credited for the excellent sailors it has produced and the boats its ex-apprentices have designed. On Sjaelland, north of Elsinore, are a couple of snug harbors, Snekkersten and Gilleleje, where fishing craft outnumber yachts.

Great cruising grounds abound along the coasts and islands around Sjaelland, as well as along the east coast of Jutland, where wooded fjords cut far inland. In the south there is a popular cruising area bordered by the islands of Funen and Langeland that continues into the Flensburger Fjord.

ARNE MAGNUSSEN

C. D.

ANDERS HOEGH POST

E.

ANDERS HOEGH POST

A. Kronborg Castle, Elsinore
B. Nyhavn, Copenhagen
C. Langelinie, Copenhagen, home of the Little Mermaid
D. Typical church, Jungshoved
E. Funen Regatta, Fyns Hoved

BAD NYT

A.

B.

Denmark's second largest city, Arhus in Jutland, is also a splendid seaport. Its history dates back 1000 years. The harbor is interesting because of the shoreside attractions of the Old Town, with its colorful half-timbered, thatch-roofed houses constructed in the 1700-1800s and its churches and museums. The old boat harbor lies to the north of town, and the new marina at Marselisborg to the south will soon be completed.

The island of Bornholm is a topographical anomaly to the rest of Denmark. Most of Denmark is barely above sea level, yet Bornholm, rising so beautifully with its dunes, hills and granite cliffs is like a different country. The sweet village of Gudhjem is famous for its smoked fish.

A few miles off Bornholm is an idyllic island called Christiansø. Originally a fort, the battlements serve as containers for vines and flowers today. The little village is charming and if you sail there, you will have made a trip that most Danes never make.

ANDERS HOEGH POST

A. Christiansø off Bornholm
B. Gudhjem Harbor, Bornholm
C. Fjallbacka, Sweden
D. Stockholm Harbor

SWEDEN

Like Norway, Sweden is wrapped in an infinity of cruising possibilities. North of Göteborg, Marstrand is a favorite yachting headquarters in the middle of the cruising triangle formed by Copenhagen, Oslo Fjord, and Stockholm. It is an island city containing grand vestiges of the past. Sailors convene here to raise their sails towards a host of scenic fishing villages, such as Smögen and Fjällbacka or Tistlarne.

The Göta Canal transverses Sweden's lake district, from the North Sea at Goteborg to the Baltic. The journey through the canal is gentle and leisurely, inviting dalliance in the inlets along the way. The Swedish countryside is sprinkled with neat little gingerbread farms and fishing camps that look like tidy dollhouses in the wilderness. There are many attractions enroute, such as the Bohus Fortress, the Trollhatten Falls and Vadstena Castle. The canal flows into the Baltic Sea at Norrköping, where various routes lead into Stockholm.

BILL ROBINSON

C. D.

ALAIN GUILLOU

BAD NYT

A.

B.

BAD NYT

C.

BAD NYT

My favourite harbour is located on the island of "Tistlarne." This little island with its lagoon is situated on the southernmost part of the Swedish West Coast archipelago. The narrow inlet to the lagoon limits the size of sailboats to approximately 30 feet. It is a natural harbour with nothing more to it than a small jetty and some sanitary arrangements. It's not very crowded most of the year in contrast to many of the bigger harbours on the Swedish West Coast.

Pelle Petterson
Industrial Designer/ Yacht Designer

Stockholm floats on 14 islands and is surrounded by many more. Its architecture is solid and elegant. It is a thrill to moor alongside wharves in great cities. Dinghy-travel makes most of the city's attractions accessible to the cruising yachtsman. The city is surrounded by the Baltic Sea and the large Lake Mälaren with the Royal Palace overlooking the confluence of the two.

Gamla Stan is the old district which originated as a Viking island fortress 700 years ago. Towers and turrets survive from that era, embellished by spires, domes and mansard roofs from more recent centuries. It is a colorful and lively town with narrow cobbled lanes winding uphill to tiny squares and fountains. The Swedish Academy, whose members select the Nobel Prize Winner for literature, is located near The Stortorget, the oldest square in Stockholm.

The island of Djurgården in Stockholm accommodates a variety of parks and open spaces, including the outdoor amusement center of Skansen. This served as the prototype for Colonial Williamsburg in Virginia. It has collected historic houses, shops, barns, and windmills from all over Sweden and re-erected them around the slopes of a zoo. The park has the requisite old-fashioned tradesmen, as well as a circus, a theatre, aquarium, indoor museums and a host of other attractions.

Of interest to seafaring folk is the 17th century warship, the *Wasa*. This barque, which was built at great expense, sank unceremoniously in the harbor on her launching day in 1628. In 1956, she was refloated, found to be remarkably well-preserved and since then has been lovingly restored.

The archipelago of Stockholm continues out into the Baltic. Sandhamn, on the seaward extremity, is a yachting center and supply station.

The walled city of Visby, on the island of Gotland, is a charming harbor whose history has revealed contacts with Minoans and the ancient Greeks. Visby was a capital of Europe during the 12th century, and the magnificent wall and some of the churches date from that time. Roses bloom through October on Gotland, adding color to an already enchanting place.

D

FINLAND

Secluded cruising awaits the sailor in the Åland Islands of Finland, which are among 6500 islands and skerries where one can get rapturously lost. The word 'aland' is the etymological grandparent of 'island.' These islands were densely populated in prehistoric times; archaeologists have found traces of 10,000 distinct settlements in this archipelago. Today, there are a few islands dotted with farms, and the total population is only 23,000. These Finns who are proud of their autonomy mainly speak Swedish.

Any sailor worth his salt knows that Finland is the birthplace of Nautor, the company that builds the exceptionally high-quality, high-performance "Swan" sailing yachts. Swan owners might enjoy a pilgrimage to Pietarsaari, the Nautor yard. Olle Emmes of Nautor has written about one of his favorite destinations, Mariehamn.

Mariehamn, the lovely little capital of the Åland Islands, sits astride a peninsula between two harbors. This port was extremely active in the grain trade, dating back to the days when fully-rigged ships rounded the Horn. Maritime history pervades the town, including remnants of warehouses, stores and supply service fragments attendant upon such a trade. The four masted bark, *Pommern*, is restored and lies in the main harbor near the Maritime Museum.

The Åland Islands are situated in the middle of the Baltic, halfway between Finland and Sweden. The entire archipelago has terrific sailing waters and Mariehamn, in the centre, is Åland's only town.

In the summer Mariehamn is a colourful place and the atmosphere almost international as the islands are visited by thousands of pleasure boats every year. The harbour of Mariehamn is not a big one, but thanks to the kindness and the excellent organizing abilities of the people who live there, things always run smoothly.

What especially fascinates me about sailing in the Finnish Archipelago – including the Åland Islands – are the "white" nights in the early part of the summer when it hardly gets dark at all.

Olle Emmes
President, "Nautor"
Pietarsaari, Finland

A. Sandhamn, Sweden
B. Göta Canal, Sweden
C. Åland Islands, Finland
D. Nautor "Swan" regatta

SOUTH AMERICA & ANTARCTICA

HAL ROTH

To reach Ca
into the wildern
would be to fol
to Elefantes Gul
ern end is the
placid lake of
greens. It is shel
which reflects i
dominated by a
blinding mounta
tinues underwat

A loud roar
warning signals
glacier calve and
surface. The noi
and dwindles to
roar, the scene s
and avenues of a

Page 229: Salvad
A. B. Cargo vesse
Chile
C. Castro, Isla Ch
D. Pala Fitos, Cas

CHII

The arc
Chile is dr.
extending fc
against the A
ern perimete
on the west.
versally by
fjords, cana
draped in lu:
this territor
ciers, waterf
canos. The
drinking wat
ity of its sea

Puerto M
watermaze ca
is the termi
last stop for
ized means
population o
center for th
the Andean
island of Chi
islands to th

A brisk
surprisingly
sloops. These
black-tarred
and are inv
produce, lum
Furthermore,
carry a horde
a region of
custom is to
where they e
their flat bott
out, unloadin

Hal Roth
number of th
the channels,
seaworthiness
mariners.

Isla Chilc
population be
into a wildern
fjords. Tidy fi
hills and chur
There are inn
several village
pilings. Castr
Chiloe.

BOB BROUSARD

A.

NED GILLETTE

B.

I had always wanted to visit Antarctica, but when I went, I was determined to go by a means no one else had ever employed. I decided to go by rowboat. In February and March 1988, I and three others crossed the Drake Passage in a 28-foot, self-righting ocean-rowing boat dubbed "Sea Tomato." We were capsized three times and flung into frigid waters. All was not daring-do; we planned carefully to leave the Cape Horn Coast on a rare northeast wind, then ride the prevailing westerlies to the South Shetland Islands. It worked. Of all my expeditions on all seven continents, this was the one on which I felt completely embraced by raw, untamed, primal nature.

Ned Gillette
Photo Journalist/Explorer

ANTARCTICA

Drake's Passage is the wild strip of ocean which separates the southern tip of South America from the northern tip of Antarctica. This stretch of water has been the passageway of many remarkable sailors and adventurers. In Drake's Passage, ships encounter icebergs as big as castles. These icebergs have a spirit of their own. When they reach Antarctica they frequently travel into harbors at amazing speed and have been known to harass boats or trap them against shore.

Antarctica is the coldest, windiest, most remote and alien place on earth. The scenery can be magnificent, colorful, otherworldly, but all accounts of voyages there speak of the brutal reality of the climate. It is interesting to note that coal deposits and fossils of lizards and reptiles found there prove that it was a more temperate place 200 million years ago.

Today, Antarctica is the home of great colonies of seals, penguins and seabirds. The surrounding waters are extremely important in world ecology as a nutrient factory for fish and marine mammals. The Antarctic Peninsula (the tail of islands that reach into Drake's Passage) is the site of a small ambassadry of scientific stations. This is the only part of the continent that is relatively ice-free part of the year. Reid Stowe, Antarctic adventurer, sailed his schooner *Anne* from New Zealand to Antarctica in 1987. He reported great camaraderie with the base crew on visits to the Russian, Argentine and American bases. He and his crew were continuously having to stand anchor watch and ease lines or weigh anchor to avoid a charging iceberg.

To date, a spirit of international scientific cooperation has triumphed over national territorial claims to pie-segments of Antarctica with no one nation claiming it for their flag. Natural resources are so inaccessible that individual territorial rights are not yet contentious. The primary resource of this continent is the knowledge it may hold for understanding climate, wildlife and the continental drift.

In view of this, leaders of Third World Nations have suggested that the Antarctic, as well as the world's seabed, be managed as the "common heritage of mankind."

Reports from Antarctica are fraught with terrifying accounts of tremendous winds and days of blinding horizontal snow. It is an environment quite alien to human survival.

Nonetheless, there seems to be a handful of intrepid mariners who find it exhilarating to try and conquer this territory.

D.

BOB BROUSARD

February 21st, 1987, Antarctica. It is my anchor watch once again. The night hours are getting longer. A heavy snow cloud shields the early dawn light and darkness envelops the glacial surroundings. There is neither sound nor movement on the boat or outside. The water is still and the icebergs that did manage to drift in have steadied in our calm spot out of the current. A thin sheet of ice has molded them into place around the schooner. Two inches of snow cover the boat, making her indistinguishable from her surroundings. Our ropes and gear on deck are hidden by the snow and frozen stiff. As dawn breaks the sea birds and penguins awake and begin their chatter. The thawed water from the glacier trickles out and pitter-patters as it drips into the sea. This anchorage, very strange and different, is labeled "Water Boat Point" on the chart. Two young Englishmen wintered over at Water Boat Point in the first part of the century, living in a small boat that was grounded on the shore. From their story and photos, I think they had a good time. The scenery is beautiful enough here.

C.

BOB BROUSARD

Port Lockroy was written up in the British Antarctic Publication as being one of the most secure anchorages in the Antarctic. The harbour is well protected by a rock and mud bottom. Here, we felt safe from the large pieces of roving sea ice; however, sometimes the 200-foot-high wall of ice would collapse, filling the bay with large chunks of ice that made it impossible to move the boat. These would grind by the hull without causing any damage. Sixty-knot winds off the glacier would eventually clear the bay. The water pouring into the bay (from the glacier) was constantly thundering.

The Melchoir Island Anchorage is situated in a very well-protected natural rock cove. Because of the rock bottom and lack of swinging room we tied off to the rocks that were exposed at the top of the high-tide mark. The rest of the land was covered with permanent ice. A penguin rookery and an abandoned British base made this a very scenic and interesting anchorage. There was access to the ice cap over a more stable part of the glacier.

Paradise Harbour has an abandoned Chilean base and is an extremely beautiful place but is one of the worst anchorages we stopped at. We always left half of the crew on the boat and the other half carried a hand-held radio and some survival gear. We tried to set our anchor on a deep rocky bottom but we never got a grip. The glacier kept the anchorage full of icebergs and we finally moved when the wind picked up.

Reid

Reid Stowe
Artist/ Adventurer

A. Old Palmer Station, Antarctica
B. Rowing to Antarctica
C. Whalers' Bay, Deception Island
D. Paradise Harbor

HAL ROTH

A.

B.

DANA JINKINS

C.

BRAZILIAN TOURISM FOUNDATION

BRAZIL

Rio de Janeiro is an exuberant city overflowing with life and personality. Situated in a fabulous natural setting, and protected by the expanse of Guanabara Bay, the city sprawls and straggles up the valleys between steep green peaks. The Pao de Acucar (Sugarloaf Mountain) that rises from a peninsula in the bay, and the Corcovado (statue of Christ the Redeemer) are landmarks that overlook the entire panorama.

Remarkable white sand beaches are in the center of town. Names like Copacabana and Ipanema have been popularized by songs reinforcing the notion that all the *Cariocas* (residents of Rio) think about is the beach. Brazilians do have an enormous capacity for enjoyment — after the beach comes soccer and samba. Fabulous dance troupes called *escolas de samba* perform in opulent costumery for many events throughout the year culminating in the annual Carnaval. Rio definitely deserves a visit, but after spending a few days there, it's nice to get away from the crowds.

Cruising in Ilha Grande Bay provides just the antidote for the bustle of Rio. It is southeast of Rio where the forests of Serra do Mar come right down to the sea and 300 paradisical islands beckon. Here and there a waterfall cascades to the sea. On the mainland, there is the charming colonial town of Parati, where high-tide washes the cobblestone streets clean daily.

Bahia de Salvador exudes a strong African influence and is famous for its warm climate, beaches, and festivals. From November right through *Carnaval* in February, the beat goes on, with dances and processions occurring regularly on the streets and at sea.

In this dense country of few roads and many rivers, boats have always been the primary mode of transportation. The colorful annual feast of Iemenjá (the goddess of the sea), takes place on the 2nd of February.

For 400 years, the *saveiro*, a beautifully crafted fishing vessel, has been used for sailing around the horn of Brazil. Burdened with culture as well as cargo, its original design came over

D.

E.

from Portugal, with some influence from Portuguese colonies in Africa. Initially the vehicle of all transoceanic trade and cargo in the extensive Portuguese colonial network, the *saveiro* has survived in Brazil, serving many purposes. These traditional boats are a symbol of migration, movement and commerce which have figured prominently in the folklore and literature of northeastern Brazil.

The *saveiros* are increasingly in demand as yachts, which overshadows their original function. They are built out of various local woods. Jatibebe, a hard red wood, is used for the hull, sicopira for the keel, olindi (a light cedar) for the decks, cunduru or beriba for the masts and jacaranda for the interiors. There is a boatbuilding yard in Valenca which specializes in these crafts. The hull and rig take many forms; the yacht version is often schooner-rigged and called an *escuña*.

Olinda, near Recife is a colonial port. Baroque buildings climb up steep streets from the harbor, and for many months of the year, the fever of dance is in the air, emphasizing the styles of *frevo* and *maracatú*.

A. Rio de Janeiro by night
B. 'Saveiros' in Valenca
C. Bahia, Brazil
D. E. Ilha Grande

I have been sailing for 30 years and I have raced in the South Atlantic, the Channels, the Caribbean, the North Atlantic and many other seas.

My vocation and avocation is the sea. Every sea-faring voyage is a search for a port: either a port of call, an anchorage or the last mooring. I mean by that the place where we want to stop, stay and grow old. Many years ago I found it at the Ilha Grande, a large stretch of land (25 miles long by 5 miles wide), facing on one side the Atlantic Ocean and on the other side the Bay of Angra dos Reis.

When I arrived there 20 years ago, nature was untouched and the high mountains, 3000 feet up from the ocean, were completely covered by dense Atlantic rain forest. The only inhabitants (something like three-to-four-thousand) depend basically on the sea and a little bit of tourism for their survival. Thanks to the efforts of a group of conscientious conservationists, it has remained untouched to this day.

My anchorage is there, in front of my house. It is a national monument and the third oldest house in the country. It was built by a Spanish pirate in 1629 and has been safe-guarded from destruction by distance and the difficulties of getting there.

As I am not of a socializing nature, I do not normally have many visitors, except sailors, who by tradition are welcome there.

What troubles me about my home anchorage is that for a place to get older it has an inconvenience: when I am there I get younger.

Israel

Israel Klabin/ Brazilian Yacht Owner
Winner of Buenos Aires/Rio Race
Former Captain of the Brazilian Team at the Admiral's Cup

GRENADA

The island of Grenada is yet another luxuriant paradise, this one especially fragrant and glowing with blossoms and spice. The perfect natural harbor of St. George's, garlanded with greenery and pastel houses with cheerful red roofs makes it probably the most eye-pleasing harbor in all the Windward Islands. The Carenage is inside the shelter of Fort George, and a marked pass leads into an even tighter lagoon where the marinas are.

There is a harmonious, integral appeal here that stems from a healthy balance of tourism with the rest of the economy which includes a strong foundation in agriculture, particularly nutmeg and spices. Despite the notorious "invasion" of U.S. troops in recent years following political turmoil, Grenada seems to be doing just fine. The lower section of St. George's bustles with noise, activity and the usual Caribbean coefficient of fumes and dirt. The residential part of town strolls up the hill amongst tree-lined lanes and colorful houses.

The Grenadians are a good-natured, spirited, opinionated people who sing a lively calypso. The island is large and merits an overland tour to get acquainted with its waterfalls, vistas, and rainforest. Prickly Bay and Spice Island Marina around the south end of the island are more comfortable than St. George's for cruising yachts.

JEFF FISHER

A.

B.

JEFF FISHER

C.

DANA JINKINS

D.

DANA JINKINS

THE GRENADINES

The Grenadines are a string of beautiful islands belonging partially to Grenada but mostly to St. Vincent. Carriacou and Petit Martinique are the only two populated islands that come under the jurisdiction of Grenada.

The St. Vincent Grenadines that are inhabited include: Bequia, Mustique, Canouan, Mayreau, Palm Island, Union and Petit St. Vincent. There is blue-water sailing here, unspoiled islands and posh resorts. A relaxed cruise in the Grenadines could take a year!

Page 241: Paget Farm, Bequia
A. St. George's Harbor, Grenada
B. Grand Anse Beach, Grenada
C. Old Plantation, Grenada
D. Just caught one! Grenada
E. Beach combing at Palm Island with Union Island in the background
F. Tobago Cays, Grenadines

KENNETH MITCHNICK

E.

F.

DANA JINKINS

MARTINIQUE

The busy port of Fort de France bustles with all kinds of craft, lots of people and far too much commercial activity for the run of most cruising needs. This extremely cosmopolitan city merits a visit for the joys of contrast and consumption. Here you can find coffee-colored beauties wearing frills of Madras, lean fishermen in their long boats and large hats and a market filled with delectables. And for those who have been dining from the sea, the ship's larder, and the sparse "biwi" grocer, an expedition to Martinique is always a culinary feast. High fashion and *haute cuisine* do come with high prices here. Martinique is a *départe-ment*, not a colony, of France and the French government is determined to build high standards of living in its *outremer*. The citizens of Martinique are wealthy by Caribbean standards.

The island lives in the shadow of an active volcano, Mont Pelée, whose last eruption in 1902 caused enormous devastation and loss of life (30,000 people). The eruption was said to be the fulfillment of a curse invoked by the Carib Indians, ruthlessly exterminated here by the European settlers in the 1600s.

Napoleon built a large stone drydock in this capital of *La Nouvelle* France to refit the ships that were defending the Tricolor in these waters. This grand edifice is the most historical place in the West Indies in which to paint your hull. When the sea recedes and the barnacly bottom of your boat is keel deep in quagmire, you might find yourself in the company of French navy destroyers and cargo vessels.

Empress Josephine, the philandering consort of the equally wayward Napoleon, was born across the bay of Fort de France at Trois Ilets. This bay, and Anse Mitan, just around a headland to the east, make for a more pleasant anchorage after you have cleared and provisioned in Fort de France.

A. Anse d'Arlet, Martinique
B. Typical fishing "pirogue"
C. Creole veranda
D. Napoleon's Fort, Îles des Saintes
E. F. Grand Bourg Harbor, Îles des Saintes

ANDRE S/Y NATCHEZ

A.

FRANK PIAZZA

B.

FRANK PIAZZA

C.

ÎLES DES SAINTES

The outer islands of Guadeloupe are literally off the beaten track. Sailors heading north from Dominica would not as a matter of course stop there. In fact, between these islands and the western coast of Guadeloupe there is a phenomenon dubbed the "Guadeloupe calm" that has frustrated more than one passing ship. Still, with appealing names like Îles des Saintes, Marie-Galante and La Desirade, you can't help but be curious about them.

Columbus named the cluster of islands that form Îles Des Saintes on "All Saints Day." There are four major islands and six smaller ones in this group. The small archipelago of "the Saints" forms a distinctive cultural anomaly. The islanders are Breton fishermen. The shy women do intricate needlework, a tradition from the Old World. Very little intermarriage with black West Indians has maintained their Breton descendancy, and kept their numbers small. Bits of gingerbread trim adorn the fading brilliance of a simple, friendly port village. Market day here offers extra delights — little cakes, a choice of salad greens, Breton fishing hats and carved bateaux.

FRANK PIAZZA

D.

E.

FRANK PIAZZA

F.

FRANK PIAZZA

ROE ANN WHITE

A.

B.

DANA JINKINS

ANTIGUA

When the Revolutionary War was raging in America, the Caribbean Sea became a strategic and active theater for naval battles among the French, Spanish and English.

British Admiral Horatio Nelson rose to fame at this time. As a young mariner he had so distinguished himself in the campaign against the American colonies that he was promoted to Captain at age 19, and soon after was given command of his own fleet. He presided over several battles in the Caribbean and married a lovely lass from Nevis.

One of the Caribbean's finest natural harbors sheltered Nelson's fleet between volleys and subsequently was named after him. Admiral Nelson's Dockyard, English Harbor, Antigua, is today an outstanding port facility to the yachting trade.

The well-preserved period buildings and flourishing shipyard provide service and social headquarters for much of the Caribbean charter fleet. The old stone sail loft building (still in use), the Copper and Lumber Stores (now a charming inn and restaurant), the Officers' Quarters (now boutiques and shops), The Admiral's Inn (the favorite watering hole) combine to create an aesthetic and practical yachting center. The whole area has been designated a National Park.

Remnants of fortresses litter this and other British West Indian islands, a reminder of Britain's seafaring empire. These islands have not known such importance in the 200 years that have since elapsed. But the wealth that floats in and out of English Harbor on pleasure craft these days could likely compete with the exchequers of empires in the 18th century.

Deadlines, deals, advertising — it can all clutter the brain — makes reminiscing about English Harbor a welcome distraction. Antigua Sailing Week is, without fear of contradiction, the empyrean Bacchanal, a madcap mélange of Disneyworld, Mardi Gras, and Fasching gone to sea. It's a sabbatical in the sun — seven days of partying, drinking, yarning, playing, and (perish the thought) racing.

You can wallow in boats and beauties galore — women are there in awesome abundance doing what they know best, which in this case means sailing and trimming and changing spinnakers with the best of men.

This single week is a compelling attraction year after year but English Harbor, offering perfect protection, and unsurpassed aesthetics, is consistently seductive.

Jeff Hammond
Publisher/ Power And Motoryacht Magazine

A. Ruins of fort at English Harbor
B. Lunch on the patio of Admirals' Inn
C. View of English Harbor from Shirley Heights
D. Dickenson Bay, Antigua

ALANNA FAGAN

C. D. E.

ALANNA FAGAN

ALANNA FAGAN

Though it brings some tears and anger, the wind of progress still allows us to roam the oceans of the world freely.

For many cruising people, St. Barts has always been an oasis of peace and friendship. Thanks to the lovely St. Barts people.

Lou Lou Magras
Loulou's Marine, Gustavia
Sailor/ Merchant

THOMAS KAUL

A.

B.

THOMAS KAUL

C.

DANA JINKINS

D.

KELVIN JONES

ANGUILLA

Somewhere, Anguilla

I believe for some time my favorite harbor was known to recreational sailors only through Carleton Mitchell, who discovered this "secret" harbor, photographed it and created a world-wide guessing game by refusing to give either its name or location. By now, alas, it seems too well known, carved by the sea out of towering cliffs on the southeast coast of Anguilla. The cove is alive with plunging pelicans and every manner of wildlife in the air and beneath its clear azure water. At sunrise, gregarious local fisherman embark in small boats. Truly a combination of serenity and active natural beauty. I won't mention its name, lest it become even more popular with sailing vessels than it already is.

Richard M. Clurman
Journalist/ Author

Somewhere, Anguilla

I think my favorite little harbor is the one on the west side of Anguilla but the trouble is I am isolated where I write this letter and can't give you the exact name of it. It would not be a very good harbor against a westerly which fortunately doesn't often happen in that part of the world.

William F. Buckley Jr.
Yachtsman/ Author
Editor, *National Review*

VIRGIN ISLANDS

St. John is the least crowded most casual member of the U.S. Virgin Islands. There seems to be a cult of Caribbean travelers who repeatedly go to St. John and have no desire to venture anywhere else. The Rockefellers have secured a large section of the island for a natural preserve, and Caneel Bay is an exclusive resort.

Round Bay is one of the largest protected harbors with several anchorages. Hurricane Hole is about as idyllic as they come. If you are looking for a marina that has a congenial cruising yacht atmosphere, facilities for provisioning and a sail loft, Coral Bay is one of the nicest around.

The British Virgin Islands contain a wealth of anchorages around Tortola — Peter Island, Salt, Cooper, Ginger, Beef and The Last Resort, a tiny private resort on the eastern edge of Tortola. One of the most unique attractions is on Virgin Gorda. A geological spasm which thrust up a maiden's form accounts for the name bestowed on this island by Columbus. Virgin Gorda's most prominent feature today is an area called The Baths, another consequence of this phenomenon. A rain of enormous boulders fell pell mell upon an otherwise normal beach, creating a fascinating network of sunlit caves, tunnels, passages and private palm beaches. A bountiful reef with grottoes and caverns flourishes underwater where the boulders came to rest. At the north end of the island there is better holding at Biras Creek and Bitter End.

Over the years, my writing assignments have taken me to many of the world's great cruising areas, from the Aegean to Australia and Newfoundland to New Zealand, with way stops in between. In the immediate aftermath of a cruise, a harbor in any one of these areas could rate as the favorite of the moment, but there is one place I always return to, the British Virgin Islands, and of all its attractive anchorages, Gorda Sound is our top choice. In 12 years of basing in the British Virgin Islands for up to five months at a time, it is the one harbor I head for most often.

While perhaps not the most exotic area, Gorda Sound is at the top for consistency of weather, ease of operation, availability of service and facilities, and a perfect layout for relaxed cruising. It is virtually landlocked, with the main approach through dramatic reefs. In anything short of a hurricane it offers perfect protection – we have comfortably ridden out a 50-knot gale in the lee of its hills. Its scenery is gracefully pleasing, and it is fine for diving, beaching, dinghy-sailing and eating ashore. We first saw it in 1964 when we were the only boat in its two-by-three mile expanse and the only houses were in the native village of Gun Creek. Now there are some 50 to 100 boats at anchor every day, and four resorts, Bitter End Y.C., Biras Creek, Leverick Bay and Drake's Anchorage.

All this is a testament to its appeal, and the recommended drill in a British Virgin Island cruise is to head east for it early on (always a challenging beat against the prevailing trades), spend a day or two enjoying Gorda Sound's delights, and then have an easy slide back to the major bases of Tortola and St. Thomas. We always enjoy a casual "boat-seeing" jog under reduced canvas around the anchorage when we first arrive, and we mix our stay between socializing and meals at Bitter End with quiet seclusion under the lee of Prickly Pear Island. Gorda Sound has just about everything a cruising stop can offer.

Bill Robinson
Contributing Editor
Cruising World Magazine

A. B. The Baths, Gorda Sound
C. Somewhere, Anguilla
D. Safely anchored in St. Johns

RICK MALOOF

RICK MALOOF

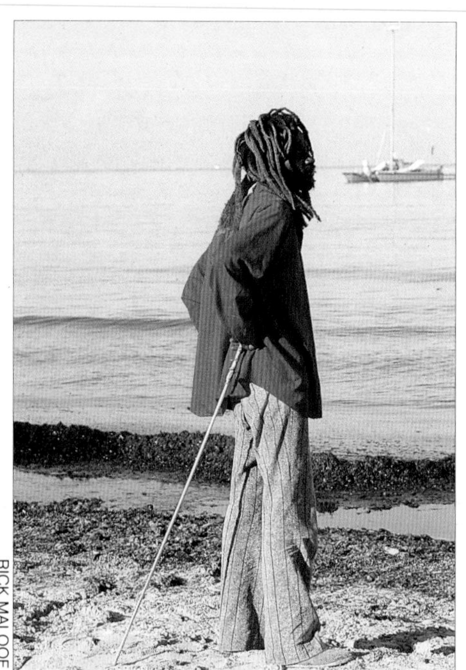

RICK MALOOF

RICK MALOOF

RICK MALOOF

RICK MALOOF

JAMAICA

Jamaica appears to be an island unto itself. Off in the western Caribbean, it's not on the cruising sailor's north-south "milk run." Still, its beauty and diversity have been a draw since well before Captain Cook brought his first breadfruit there from the South Pacific. Jamaica, the third largest Caribbean island, is lush with vegetation, rivers, waterfalls and voluptuous mountains. Arriving from sea after spending time in the low-lying Bahamas, one sailor was impressed by what appeared to be a huge black cloud on the horizon. The cloud turned out to be the famous Jamaican Blue Mountains.

Colonials and half of Hollywood have had vacation houses in Jamaica for years, but tourism dwindled in the 1960s with reports of political and social problems. The Jamaican Tourist Board is working overtime to entice visitors back to Jamaica and is doing a great job of it.

Montego Bay and Kingston, of calypso fame, need only be a stop of convenience for marine facilities. The sweat of the city and the high decibel level emitted from the "Rasta boxes" (known as ghetto blasters in the streets of New York) are not enchanting. To its credit, Jamaica is the home of "reggae" and the birthplace of Bob Marley. The offbeat music not only permeates all of the Caribbean, but has been musically influential world-wide. It's great to dance to, but doesn't go with cornflakes in your cockpit at breakfast.

Negril, once a low-key languid beach has been growing in leaps and bounds. The seven miles of sugar-white sand are a shell collector's paradise. Tents and lean-tos have been replaced by large-capacity hotels. Boats can anchor off the beach once they make their way in through the coral reef which protects Negril, but there is no harbor here.

Port Antonio is still relatively quiet, catering to both local fishing craft and sportfishing boats. There are many sportfishing competitions that take place out of this pleasant harbor. People are "coming back" to Jamaica, and with good reason.

HAITI

Making port in Haiti is not as fearful a proposition as it may appear from afar. It is a desperately poor country, but like many Third World countries, the people exhibit a style and a fortitude, mingled with mischief and magic, that helps them through their strife. Haiti remains an intriguing place. There is a colorful exotica of Africa which is more evident here than in the rest of the Caribbean.

The rich and beautiful colony filled French and Spanish coffers handsomely until 1800 when the colonial slaves and mulattos got wind of the French Revolution and started a rebellion themselves. The white world was shocked when valorous statesmen and military geniuses rose from the ranks of slavery to successfully overthrow the French colonial power structure and declare nationhood for the Black Republic of Haiti. Unfortunately, the new powers were not immune to corruption and delusions of grandeur. This impressive fight for freedom deteriorated into a sad *dénouement*. The opportunism of practically all its subsequent leaders has caused Haiti to be deforested and ransacked of its resources.

As the world must know, Haiti has had and continues to have its unfair share of problems — politically, socially and economically. Pleasure cruising in Haiti might seem an anathema. However, we have had more than one account of good experiences there. Personally, I find Labadie to be one of the most beautiful anchorages in the region. The harbor is circular with steep cliffs overlooking the crystal clear waters. There is a primitive village nearby and the snorkeling here is wonderful.

RICK MALOOF

A. B.

RICK MALOOF

C.

MATTHEW TOTH

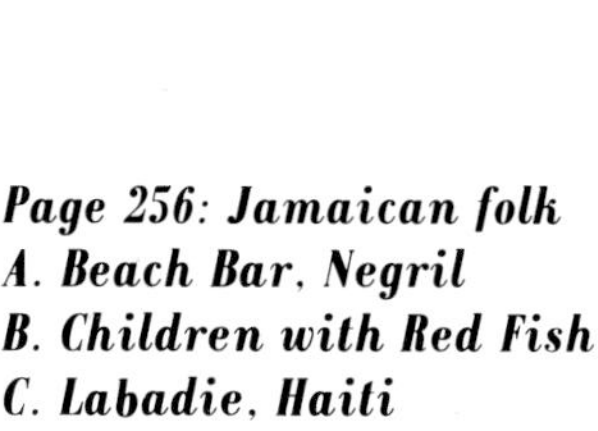

Page 256: Jamaican folk
A. Beach Bar, Negril
B. Children with Red Fish
C. Labadie, Haiti

BAHAMAS to the CHESAPEAKE & BERMUDA

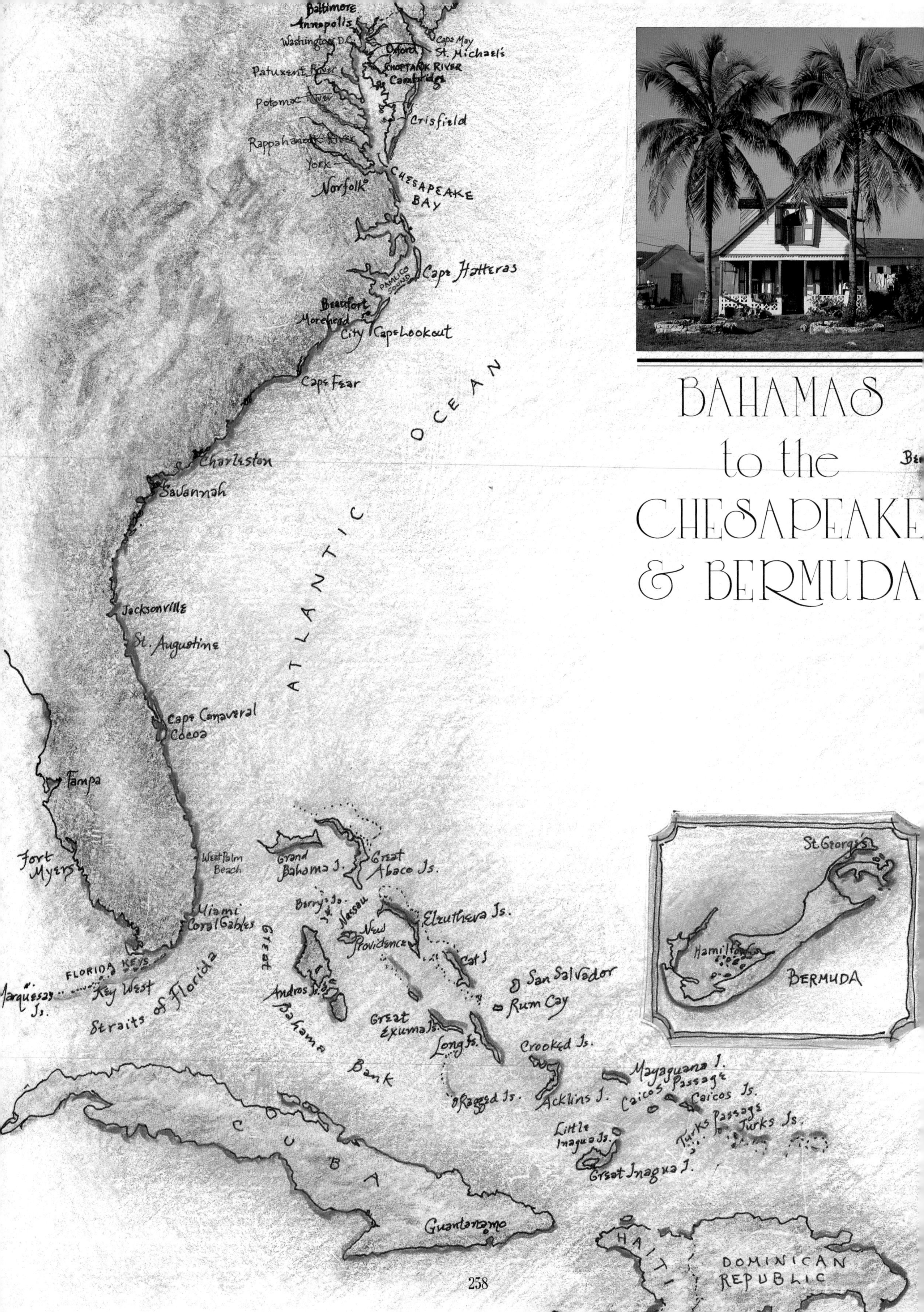

FRANK PIAZZA

A. B.

DANA JINKINS

William Grey, a freed slave living on Long Island in the 1870s, had clung to the floating timbers of his ship-wrecked Bahamian smack for nearly eight days on the waters of Exuma Sound before he washed up on the windward shore of Staniel Cay. But he wasn't the first to taste the sweet, pure water from the two natural wells, or to quickly see that the "cut" from deep Exuma Sound onto the Banks was easily navigable, thus offering a protected inside passage to Nassau. Ponce de Leon first explored the "Yumeys" (Exumas) in 1513, noting the same topographical advantage, as did the British in later years.

In 1962, Bob Chamberlain, a "drop out" from Los Angeles and Lockheed Corporation, sailed his charter schooner "Malabar" into Big Rock Cut, dropped an anchor, explored the island, declared that he had found "home," and the "crossroads watering hole" of the Exumas was born – the Staniel Cay Yacht Club.

All sailors and yachtsmen who ply the waters today between Florida and the West Indies must know the always-friendly, cheerful "Berkie" Rolle! For 24 years he has been the helpful dockmaster, and his wife Vivian the "mistriss" of Bahamian cooking on the island. They're all descended from William Grey and still speak of him. "Grandaddy still de head for all de goodness what he do for we." And for the sailor, the "goodness" has been the blessing of a naturally positioned island offering a safe anchorage, sweet water and navigable access through the Exumas. "Ponce, it's your turn to buy a round."

Captain Richard G. Bristol
Professional Yacht Captain

BAHAMAS

Anchorages in the Bahamian Islands are good for repose, rejuvenation and a vast panorama of sky and sea. Lacking the bold physical features or striking history that impresses us in other harbors, the beauty of the Bahamas is in their solitude, and the brilliant providence of the waters which offer some of the most magnificent snorkeling and diving in the world. Unlike the Mediterranean or the Caribbean, this sea has not been fished out. You can have grouper for breakfast, *langousta* for lunch and conch served in twenty different ways for supper.

THE EXUMAS

The Exuma Cays are a beautiful archipelago that stretches southeast from Nassau. A collection of deserted coves are interspersed with local restaurants and watering holes. The shores of these islands are graced by casuarina and lignum vitae trees. Staniel Cay is an attractive settlement with a delightful, informal yacht club. The good times here are enhanced by the superb diving in underwater caves.

The main yachting center in the Exumas is in Elizabeth Harbor between Great Exuma and Stocking Island. There is an excellent hurricane hole on Stocking Island, and several pleasant hideaways within a small radius of Georgetown. This pleasant little town is a metropolis by Bahamian standards. It is well-equipped with supplies, including several inns and pubs, most notably the pink "Peace and Plenty Club."

Every April a huge fleet of swift and sleek Bahamian fishing smacks and racing sloops gather for the Family Islands' (Out Islands) Regatta. It's a lively and raucous three-day party attended by owners of working boats from as far away as Andros, as well as great numbers of foreign yachtsmen.

Great Exuma and Long Island, along with Crooked and Acklins Islands, were hosts to some elegant cotton plantation homes. Most were demolished in the hurricane of 1926, but a few architectural remnants remain.

ELEUTHERA

Governor's Harbor, Eleuthera, is the oldest settlement in the Bahamas. A former governor of Bermuda led a group of dissatisfied adventurers here in 1649 in search of a community where they could enjoy "liberty of conscience." When they settled, he named the island Eleuthera, the Greek word for freedom. The island has many anchorages and four tidy settlements, still thriving today.

There are actually two harbors here on either side of a causeway leading to Cupid's Cay. This settlement had strong connections with New England and many Loyalists from the new United States of America resettled here. Most of the historic buildings are on Cupid's Cay.

Spanish Wells is a prosperous little community situated on a narrow cay. The town is only a few blocks wide and extremely picturesque from seaward, with palm trees swaying in the yards of red-roofed houses. The local people are good farmers and fishermen.

Page 259: Bahamian sloop
A. Elizabeth Harbor, Great Exuma
B. Playing on the beach in Eleuthera
C. Family Islands regatta, Georgetown, Exumas
D. Colonial architecture, Eleuthera

FRANK PIAZZA

C.

D.

DANA JINKINS

SUSAN SMITH

A.

B.

SUSAN SMITH

I first went to Key West in the late 70s to relax. I was exhausted from finishing a novel, and a writer friend – the late Jimmy Kirkwood – had offered me his house there. I went planning to play tennis, dive the coral reef and generally vegetate in the sun. I didn't expect to meet a town where Schwinns outnumber Fords, where the palms and flowers make you wish you studied botany, and the gingerbread-styled, two-story veranda homes inspire you to move here.

I haven't moved to Key West, but I've returned often since. Enough to feel like a native when applauding the Mallory Square sunsets, or knowing that the best fish sandwich in the world is at the Full Moon Saloon, and that whether it's at the Old Monster Disco, or the tea dances at La-Ti-Da, visitors and residents alike – gay or straight – are always on the make.

I've met Key West Hippies who still think it's 1968, and Cubans who spend their days gazing longingly 90 miles out to sea. I've been in Key West during hurricanes when we water-skiied down Duvall Street, and when the main concern in town was who got to play Hedy Lamarr. And once I bailed out a friend during Fantasy Fest (Key West's Mardi Gras), explaining to the officer that he was wearing a dress, only to be told politely that the cells held so many men in dresses that I'd have to describe his in more detail.

Tennessee Williams could have created a town like this. That he didn't have to is one of the reasons he lived here, as do so many writers and artists, and others who appreciate beauty, tolerance, sophistication, and simplicity, all on an island light years from the rest of the world.

Tom Seligson

Tom Seligson
Author/ Journalist/ Television Producer

KEY WEST

A lot of history, color and intrigue is concentrated in this small piece of the tropics at the southernmost tip of the United States. Key West has been a pirates' headquarters, a wreckers' base, a naval outpost and a fishermen's mecca. At the end of the last century when it was Florida's largest city, enormous wealth was garnered through some or all of these pursuits in order to build the beautiful homes which gracefully combine New England architecture with the modest creole cottage. Many of these estates and "Conch" houses are being rescued from crumbling decadence.

An illustrious collection of notable personalties have tied their fortunes with Key West, weaving their lives into the fabric of this oasis in the Gulf Stream. Audubon did much of his nature painting here; Hemingway's former home is now a museum and Tennessee Williams won't soon be forgotten. Singer Jimmy Buffett returns to Key West between tours. Game fishing has attracted several other contemporary writers including Jim Harrison and Thomas McGuane. And there is Mel Fisher and his team of treasure hunters who, after years of trying, finally found millions of dollars worth of treasure from the vessel, the *Atocha*, which left Havana, Cuba in 1622 and subsequently foundered and sank in the Marquesas 25 miles west of Key West.

Although its own harbor is adequate and supplies a large shrimp fleet, the enchantment of this place is on shore, at sunset, where a ritualistic sunset party occurs virtually every night on the pier. The iguana man is probably no longer there, but jugglers, acrobats, locals and tourists join together to watch the sun go down. What is most special about Key West is that it truly feels like an outpost – you can't believe you are in America. It's a town of lightheartedness and dreams.

Several marinas on auxiliary cays and islands provide more comfortable facilities for yachts. Wisteria Island at the northwest corner of Key West, (also known as Christmas Tree Island) provides convenient shelter.

SAINT AUGUSTINE

Ponce de Leon claimed to have discovered The Fountain of Youth in St. Augustine. Indeed, something intangible seems to have preserved the Hispanic tradition in a gracious unhurried style unlike most of Florida. Cruising north through Florida's Intracoastal Waterway involves long miles in flat and sometimes urban marsh, the only rewards being porpoises, manatees and a host of shorebirds. St. Augustine, the oldest town in Florida, offers more than beaches and nature.

In addition to the Spanish battlements and a restored Spanish town, there are many beautiful buildings here. Activity centers around the town square, a palm-shaded promenade in the shadow of two ornate churches. Fairs and festivals take place here.

St. Augustine's ancestry in Catholic, Mediterranean fishing ports is celebrated every spring with the Blessing of the Fleet. The commercial shrimp fleet and other boats spruce up their craft and dress ship for a parade in front of the bishop. The number of attending yachtsmen increases every year.

A. B. C. Tropical Key West
D. Flagler College, St. Augustine

SUSAN SMITH

C.

D.

WILLIAM ARNOLD

My "favorite" harbor depends on my particular needs at the time. Various and disparate criteria include: (1) A well-protected, easy-to-enter-in-all-weather, crew-change and reprovisioning stopover en route to the West Indies. (2) A real sailor's town stocked with hard-to-find supplies and hordes of talented craftsmen available at reasonable wages for rip-up, rip-out and rebuild projects. (3) A coast-wise cruising harbor where you can wile away a few days, complete with attractive village within flip-flop distance, lots to do shorewise, a gregarious transient sailing crowd and grog shop tenders who don't ask you if you're actually planning to climb the North Face when you start talking about Mount Gay. (4) A lovely lagoon where you can hang out on the hook, kick sand on a mile of deserted beach, dig clams aplenty and let the rest of the world go crazy without the slightest complicity on your part.

Given some latitude, that harbor is Beaufort, North Carolina. (Criteria #4, The Lovely Lagoon, is an hour's sail up to Cape Lookout.)

Beaufort's virtues: exceptionally fine folk; well-protected from storms and an excellent location for ice-free winter layup-afloat; an extensive network of honest and talented craftsmen; quaint and historical whatzits splattered all over the place; grits, eggs and smoked Virginia ham at Mike's Restaurant for $2.95 (coffee included); seafood cheap and plentiful enough to encourage the growth of gill slits on your neck; a terrific marina with outstanding staff who don't look cross-eyed at you if your yacht isn't equipped with twin outriggers and fighting chairs; and finally, a place where you can watch wild ponies romp on sand dunes while a bugle blows evening retreat. (You gotta' admit, you don't see that sort of class act just anywhere.)

Then again, if you're really picky, there's the 79th Street Marina ...

Doug Terman
Author/ Yachtsman

BELL PHOTOGRAPHY

A.

B.

JACK M. ALTERMAN

BEAUFORT

Wild horses graze on a flat, grassy island to one side of the harbor channel at Beaufort, North Carolina (pronounced Bow-foot as opposed to South Carolina's Byew-foot). On the other bank is a pleasant harborfront of shops, restaurants and historic homes. It is a popular stopover for yachts traveling the Intracoastal Waterway, either as a place for a refit or as a launching area for a journey offshore.

This lovely little town has done an excellent job of preserving its history, in buildings as well as events. An excellent maritime museum in Beaufort illuminates some of the early life of this port and of Cape Lookout National Seashore. The fishing community supplies a number of good restaurants in town, as well as those in Morehead City across the bridge.

From here one could sail on to historic Bath or Ocracoke — or Shanghai or Zanzibar. Or go and listen to some ancient mariners who did. At Sea Level, North Carolina is Snug Harbor, a nursing home for merchant mariners who have finally "swallowed the anchor." It was there I had the pleasure of listening to the spellbinding yarns of some old sailors who had gone to sea at 14 and sailed the Tall Ships around the Horn. They told some amazing stories of their youth in the Golden Age of Sail.

CHARLESTON

Charleston is a gracious old city circumscribed by water. It was the shipping port of a large plantation network whose cargo was hauled by boat. These trade connections extended to the West Indies, influencing the population and the culture of Charleston. The Straw Market downtown that displays the splendid basketwork and other crafts is one example of Caribbean input. Antebellum plantations, with their magnificent gardens, are open to the public. There are several good marinas on either side of the peninsula of Old Charleston. Markets and restaurants, historic sights and performing arts centers in the charming old city are quite accessible. Strolling under the magnolias and live oak that grow among the beautiful homes and churches for which Charleston is famous is an entertaining diversion. Eighteenth century homes were the summer residences of the planters who came to town to socialize and escape the mosquitos.

The scenic avenues run lengthwise down to watersmeet at Battery Park. This gracious promenade is the foreground for some of Charleston's prettiest homes. From here you can see the fortress on Battery Island in the middle of Charleston Bay that was the scene of several battles in the Revolutionary War. The first shots of the Civil War were fired by the Confederate Army here, reducing Fort Sumter to rubble.

CHESAPEAKE BAY

The Chesapeake Bay is a cradle of American civilization which has retained much of its history and natural charm. The bay is fed by dozens of rivers whose cumulative 6000 miles of tidewater coast and tributaries offer infinite possibilities for "gunkholing," or poking around creeks and inlets until you find yet another secret anchorage for the night.

History permeates this area. The names Yorktown and Jamestown are as familiar to foreigners as to residents. St. Mary's City, a dynamic little community, was the historic first capital of Maryland. It is situated at the mouth of the Potomac. This port is the terminus for the Governor's Cup Race, originating in Annapolis in August.

Relics of ancient natural history abound at the Calvert Cliffs on the western shore near the mouth of the Patuxent River. Fossilized sharks' teeth and other artifacts wash out of the eroding cliffs and litter the beach near Solomon's Island. The Calvert Marine Museum includes some outstanding exhibits, including the hexagonal lighthouse formerly off Drum Point.

This region of the Chesapeake is a base for estuarine scientific research. The Jefferson Patterson Park Museum is perched on a knoll overlooking St. Leonard's Creek, the site of a naval battle during the War of 1812. It is one of the prettiest anchorages in the Bay.

WILLIAM ARNOLD

C.

On the eastern shore of the Chesapeake Bay there are a myriad of rivers, creeks and streams. In the Choptank River at the confluence with the Tred Avon River lies Oxford, Maryland, a quiet little sea town. Tourism, fishing and boatbuilding are the main industries. Here, there are still a couple of active Chesapeake Bay "Bugeyes" sailing around. Oystermen "tong" for their haul, and the locals are pleased to see sailors stopping over. There is plenty of dock space and more than one excellent watering hole to frequent where you can swap nautical yarns and tall stories. Summer recreation includes racing log canoes. Another Chesapeake sport is hunting – hunters come from all over the world to stalk the migrating geese in the fall.

We had a very pleasant interlude of four months doing a major refit on the 98-foot Rhodes motorsailer "Astral" in Bachelor Point Harbor where John Todd runs a small, efficient and relaxed, but very fine boatyard specializing in top-quality workmanship. The boatyard is particularly noted for its excellent cabinet and joinery work, and attention to detail. However, do not contemplate a cruise in January – it can get very cold. We even held bicycle races on the ice in the boat basin prior to our departure. Then we had to hire a tug and barge to break our way out of the ice all the way to the Bay proper.

Oxford is a congenial, somnolent little town, and a good place to stop for a night or two to resupply, or a month or two to refit, with good access to all sorts of boat equipment – far enough away to be unhurried and yet close enough to get things done.

David and Avril Howe
Professional Yacht Captain and Charter Chef

A. Beaufort, North Carolina
B. Charlestown, South Carolina
C. St. Michael's, Maryland

THE EASTERN SHORE

The silhouette of billowing square-sails or of oyster tongers at work enhances the pleasure of cruising the Chesapeake Bay. In addition to the profusion of traditionally built pleasure craft, there is a varied fleet of native workboats: bugeyes, log sailing canoes, deadrise fishing boats, ducktails, skipjacks, and bateaux. The Chesapeake Bay Maritime Museum at St. Michael's exhibits an extensive collection of local craft.

The vessels and techniques of crab and oyster fishing in the Chesapeake are living testament to a vanishing breed. There are some 40 Chesapeake Bay skipjacks still dredging for oysters under sail, probably the last working fleet under sail in the United States. They are handsome craft, with their raked masts and clipper bows. In the autumn you can see these old beauties laden with oysters rolling home under full sail to the Choptank, Tilghman's or Smith Island.

Crisfield, Maryland is a rustic fishing port which calls itself the "Soft-Crab Capital of the World." The same "waterman" blood and surnames are found on Smith and Tangier Island near here in Tangier Sound. These small island communities have a unique and enduring character.

Sailing the rivers of the Eastern Shore is an anthropological journey to a special corner of America. Until the Bay Bridge linked the Eastern Shore to the mainland metropolis in the 1950s, the Delmarva (Delaware, Maryland and Virginia) Peninsula communities were quite isolated. As principal colonial ports in a remote region, they developed an independent economy and a strong indigenous character and vernacular. There is nobility and historic ancestry in the colonial towns of Oxford, St. Michael's and Cambridge, as well as the colorful strength of the working class.

Many skipjacks gather for the annual Workboat Race off Sandy Point around Halloween. The Eastern Shore is especially beautiful in autumn; the weather is crisp and glorious often into November and the shores of creeks and inlets are ablaze with color. With huge flocks of geese honking overhead, swans drifting along on the reflection of blue skies and brilliant crimson foliage, you couldn't ask for a finer cruising ground.

James Michener's book, *Chesapeake,* chronicles eons of history on the Choptank River. The fifth and sixth generation of some of those families can still be found at the same trades in the environs of Cambridge and Oxford.

There are excellent yachting facilities and boatyards that have been in operation for generations all along both shores of the Bay. Oxford is a delightful port with all the amenities, close to excellent gunkholing on the Tred Avon River.

A.

RICK MALOOF

B.

RICK MALOOF

C.

A. Workboats, Frenchtown, Maryland
B. Pirate's Wharf on the Wicomico River
C. Blue Crabs for dinner
D. Skipjack Somerset in Mt. Vernon Harbor
E. Wharf at Crisfield, Maryland

RICK MALOOF

D.

E.

RICK MALOOF

RICK MALOOF

MARTY KATZ

A.

B.

MARTY KATZ

C.

BILL ARNOLD

ANNAPOLIS

Annapolis, the historic port and state capital of Maryland, is the home of the U.S. Naval Academy and one of the largest concentrations of boats and boatyards on the Atlantic Coast. It is an extremely scenic and active port on the Severn River, which offers beautiful cruising. Annapolis has chandleries, sailmakers, full-service marinas, diesel mechanics — everything a sailor could need. The only difficulty is finding a berth — Annapolis is very popular!

The town center of Annapolis with its historic buildings is an architectural treat. Restaurants and bars proliferate, many of which open for a season and close. But McGarvey's has consistently good burgers and brews. The sumptuous covered market at the head of the city dock offers a European approach to fresh produce, pasta, savories and meats. The take-out fried chicken is the best north of the Mason-Dixon Line.

Cruising upriver is a delightful option in the many tributaries of the Chesapeake Bay. The Sassafras River on the upper Eastern Shore offers many beautiful anchorages surrounded by fields and forest, with the pleasant town and yachting center of Georgetown at its head.

BALTIMORE

Fifteen years ago no one would have considered Baltimore a harbor of enchantment. Baltimore Harbor has undergone a tremendous metamorphosis from a mess of old broken wharves and sunken barges to a thriving, colorful, recreational waterfront. After years of steady restoration and new construction, the Inner Harbor includes a promenade of shops, restaurants, museums and a marina.

Downriver is Fells Point, the original harbor that is situated in the oldest part of the city. It is an active ethnic community on the fringes of Little Italy and Greektown populated by an interesting amalgam of Baltimoreans: tugboat captains, *avant-garde* artists and motorcycle riders, together with their aunts and grandfathers shaking their heads from marble stoops.

BERMUDA

Bermuda is a seductive little place, a tropical island under northern skies in mid-Atlantic. Always a welcome harbor after many hundred miles at sea, the cluster of white and pastel houses against the turquoise crystal coves is story-book perfect. A sophisicated environment like Bermuda's is especially appreciated after threading your way through reefs and encountering the notoriously unpredictable weather systems. Sailors coming from the gentle havens in the tropics are often surprised by the storms created when northers mix up with the Gulf Stream. Many yachts have gone awry on the reefs surrounding Bermuda.

Bermuda is the object, the passion and the rendezvous of many racing sailors. In June, racing fleets come in from Newport, Annapolis and the West Indies, some of which will cruise on to the Azores and Europe. Around the archipelago of Bermuda itself, there are fine cruising grounds with hidden coves and tiny floral islands to explore.

There is a formality about the crown colony of Bermuda that distinguishes it from the rest of the tropics. You may be there on vacation, but businessmen in lime-green Bermuda shorts with ties and blazers are leaving their English ivy-covered cottages and going off to work!

May 24th is a big holiday. It's the first day Bermudians officially go swimming (after the mild but chilly enough winter) and there are festivities, topped off by the "fitted dinghy" races. These 14-foot open boats with very long bowsprits — 1000 square-foot of sail and enormous spinnakers — are a wonderful spectacle. There always seems to be more crew than the boat can hold hiked out on the windward rail, and one crew member whose full-time job is to bail the boat.

St. Georges is the port of preference for cruising sailors.

A. Annapolis, Maryland
B. Fells Point, Baltimore
C. Inner Harbor, Baltimore
D. Bermudian sailboats "dressed" for the 24th of May
E. St. Georges, Bermuda

BILL ROBINSON

D.

E.

IAN SPURLING

The picturesque town of St. Georges is situated at the eastern end of the Bermuda Islands. With its pastel-coloured buildings and white roofs, it was the second town built by the English in the New World. The deep-water, protected harbour has provided a safe haven for vessels for almost four centuries. Steeped in history, St. Georges boasts the oldest continually used Anglican Church in the Western Hemisphere. Many old forts, still standing, protected the town and harbour. The island was considered the turning mark for sailing ships travelling from the West Indies and the Spanish colonies. The strategic importance of Bermuda to England in the New World helped the English become a great sea power during the 18th and 19th centuries. Bermuda's past and present ties us to the sea. The people are famous for their friendliness to visiting yachts and seafarers. The clean harbour and excellent facilities ashore leave one with a memorable feeling for this town.

Steve Hollis
Sailmaker, St. Georges, Bermuda

JENNIFER CANNELL

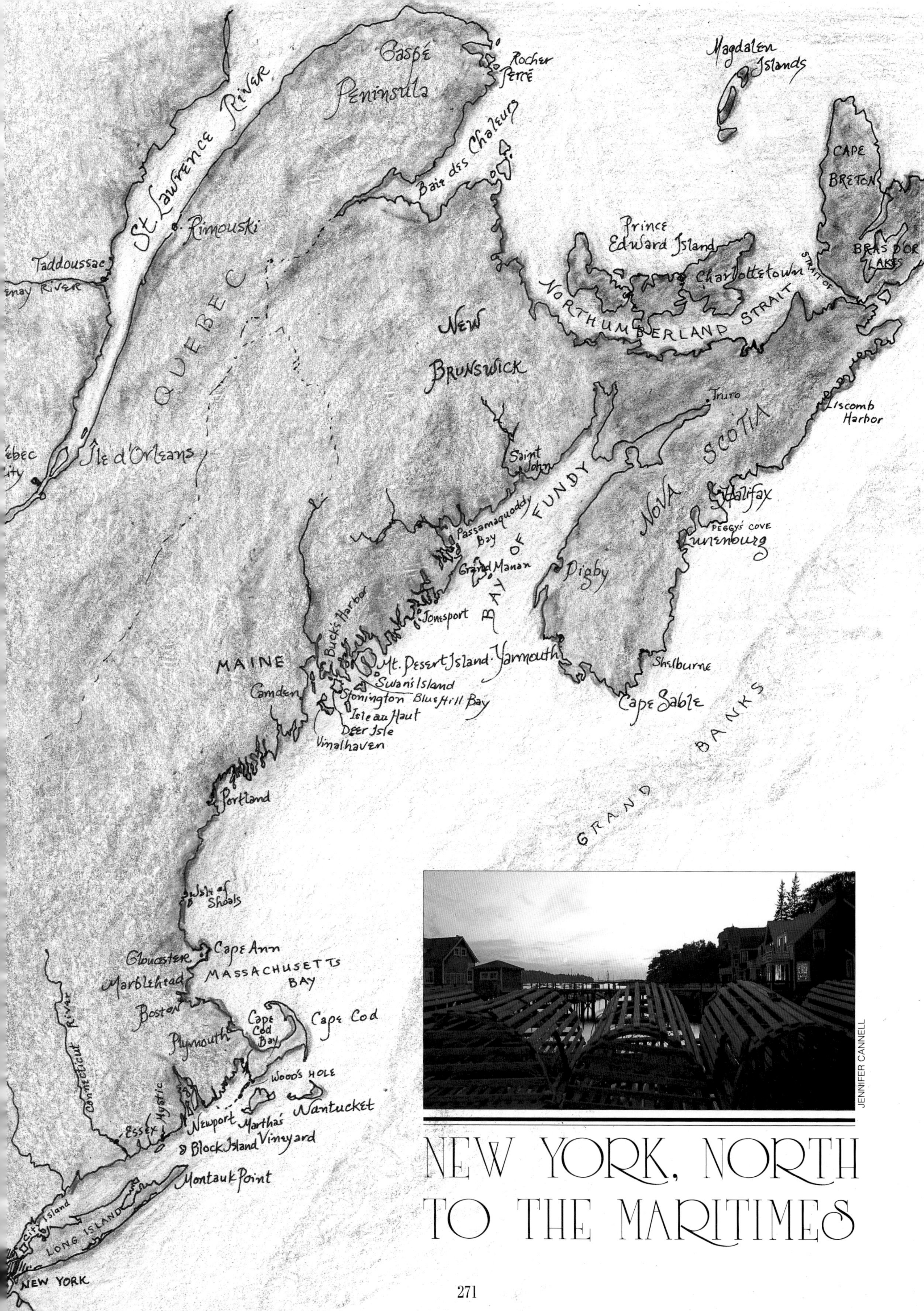

JENNIFER CANNELL

NEW YORK, NORTH TO THE MARITIMES

JOHN DONOVAN

A. B.

JAMES WALLEN

C.

STAN RIES

NEW YORK CITY

People might shake their heads at the thought of New York City as an enchanting harbor. But, transcending the negative clichés of crime, pollution and mania in that order, there are indeed positive attributes to New York Harbor. Cruising through this great seaport can be a thrill and a challenge. Sailing through the Verrazano Narrows where you behold Manhattan's peerless skyline, or cruising out of Long Island Sound through Hell's Gate up the Harlem River to the Hudson offers incomparable vistas of urban and maritime spectacle.

New York is an archipelago with coves, currents, tides and even fish — a fact easily forgotten when you are strolling down Broadway. New Yorkers with apartments on East End Avenue or Riverside Drive are fortunate enough to be aware of the constant parade of sail and powerboats, tugs and barges.

New York's historical South Street Seaport is currently being restored as an Historic Preservation Site, which includes the museum, a collection of period ships, the Fulton Fish Market, a planetarium, galleries and — promised soon — a marina for transient yachts. The historic buildings and ships' rigging are surrounded by polished granite and towers of steel and glass; the view of Lower Manhattan from the water is spectacular.

As much waterfront as surrounds New York, there are few good marinas. July, 1989 marks the opening of North Cove supermarina for megayachts. This elegant marina and office complex offers mooring facilities for high finance afloat. Others who check into New York Harbor must make do at the 23rd St. Marina, 79th St. Marina, or any number of other falling-down piers, until interested parties focus as much attention on the waterfront as they do on the Westside Highway.

Page 270: Camden Harbor, Maine
A. Lower Manhattan
B. Fishers Island
C. Hudson River sunset
D. Larchmont, N.Y.
E. Statue of Liberty, New York City

HUDSON RIVER

Man-made splendors along the Hudson River give way to natural grandeur as you cruise north. The river meanders surprisingly soon out of its urban confines into the Palisades, where it flows between steep, rounded mountains which characterize this leg of the journey until you are above Catskill Creek.

The river twists around Bear Mountain and Storm King. The majesty of this scenery inspired the Hudson River School of Painters, America's home-grown landscape artists who created a natural romantic genre of painting, free of European influence. The Highlands also inspired Washington Irving to weave the magic tale of Rip Van Winkle.

The beauty of the Hudson River is incomparable. It has many charming and historical ports, connecting via locks and canals to further harbors of enchantment in Lake Champlain, the St. Lawrence and the Great Lakes.

For me and the Forbes' "Highlander" there is no harbor more special, more spectacular, more exciting than New York itself. Awesome by day and glitteringly dazzling by night, it's the "Highlander's" "daily beat"for entertaining – getting to know the economy's makers and shakers.

Malcolm S. Forbes
Forbes Magazine
New York City

BILL ROBINSON

D. E.

STAN RIES

DANA JINKINS

A. B.

STAN RIES

C.

STAN RIES

My favorite harbor is actually a creek. It is called Selden's Creek and it leads into Selden's Pond, surrounds Selden's Island and exits back into the Connecticut River.

Offering protection, seclusion and beauty, the cliffs protecting this meandering creek are now covered with pine, moss and wildflowers. This was not always so. This was once the site of one of the largest quarries in New England. Over six-hundred men operating steam drills hauled granite to waiting schooners by way of small railways — a frontier atmosphere worked by desperate men.

It is again quiet. An osprey wheeling in the spring sky brings thoughts of Georgian Bay. It is, however, only two miles from my office in downtown Essex, Conn.

Jim Eastland

James Eastland
President, Eastland Yachts, Inc.
Essex, Connecticut

CONNECTICUT RIVER

The Connecticut River extends 410 miles from Old Saybrook, Connecticut on Long Island Sound to the Canadian border. It is navigable from the mouth of the river to Hartford, a lovely stretch where many creeks and inlets exist around places like Old Lyme, Essex, Selden's Creek and Hamburg Cove. The staunch Connecticut towns with their white church steeples and town greens and brass plaques commemorating who slept there in 1776 are each charming in their own way.

MYSTIC SEAPORT

My first journey to Mystic Seaport was an evocative trip back in time. Twilight broadened into a crimson bath and the mist rose on the river as we motored through the bascule bridge to the darkened town. The silhouettes of windvanes, boatsheds and the rigging of Tall Ships graced the evening sky. Swans glided alongside our craft. The dockmaster directed us to a berth near the *Joseph Conrad*, then helped orient us to the place. With the crowds gone and the museum closed for the day, we had the grounds all to ourselves, and the opportunity to spend an evening in the 19th century.

This living maritime museum is best visited by sea. It is a replica of the village of Mystic in the 19th century. The flotilla of historic vessels includes a whaling ship, the *Charles W. Morgan*; a fishing schooner, the *L.A. Dunton*; the *Joseph Conrad*, a square-rigged training ship; the schooner *Brilliant*, and a coal-fired steamer which takes passengers on harbor tours. In addition to this fleet, the shoreside community has all the working exhibits of a 19th century seaport, complete with an informative staff.

A. Newport, Rhode Island
B. Block Island lighthouse
C. Connecticut Shore
D. Newport, Rhode Island

Well-protected, well-located, Cuttyhunk is a perfect jumping-off place for Nantucket, Martha's Vineyard, and the Cape Cod Canal to the east, and Newport, Block Island, and Long Island Sound to the west. Cuttyhunk's Salt Pond offers total shelter from all weather,and the anchorage outside the pond is good in all but northwest through northeast wind. The island is comfortably walkable, from the compact village with buildings stacked among the ledges on one end, up the hill to the 360-degree-sweep of Buzzard's Bay, Vineyard Sound, and Rhode Island Sound, to the rolling meadows on the other end. The meadows are planted here and there with ruins of observation bunkers from the war, and you will no doubt see rather blasé deer munching, munching. Just how much they munch and how blasé they are becomes evident when you see the lengths the locals go to protect shrubs and gardens, and when you hear the the 4 a.m. crash of a garbage can lid.

Cuttyhunk is extremely popular, its closely-gridded transient moorings often holding a raft-up each. Go in spring or fall on a weekday, and enjoy a museum-like miniature island, happily stuck in a time warp.

Bill Storandt

William Storandt
Yachtsman/ Journalist

BLOCK ISLAND

The Indians called Block Island *Manisses*, the Island of the Little God. This lovely little Victorian community is only a few miles from civilization, but in peace and pace it seems as if it's a world away.

Block Island had no natural harbor, hence no whaling fleet and no fancy summer cottages. The first settlers in the 17th century were a well-educated and determined lot of 16 families fleeing the inflexible dogma of Puritanism. Liberals, intellectuals and egalitarians, they left behind careers and wealth to form a new community on the fertile hills of the harborless *Manisses*. They held the heretical views that landless people should be allowed to vote, that colonists should buy land from the Indians and that religion was not a matter of state. Furthermore, they were willing to sacrifice worldly gain for their ideals of democracy.

They survived handsomely, and their descendants went on to build a breakwater, catch fish and raise crops. The island's potential as a summer resort blossomed in the Victorian age, when a collection of large rambling hotels were built at Old Harbor on the eastern shore. Many were destroyed by a hurricane but all restorations have followed this style.

Many racing sailors convene at Great Salt Pond, to the west, for the annual Block Island Race Week. This haven is larger and unperturbed by the ferry and swarms of day-trippers.

DANA JINKINS

D.

NEWPORT

Newport is the quintessential nautical town. Over the years it has been a port of commerce, whaling, the Navy, sailing and racing. The town is endowed with historic edifices that date from colonial days through the middle of this century. Palatial mansions like the Breakers and the Marble House grace Bellevue Avenue and the Cliff Walk.

Every other June, Newport to Bermuda racers convene at the Ida Lewis Yacht Club in Brenton Cove. The Annapolis-Newport Race and the Classic Yacht Regatta take place on alternate years. And, of course, before the Australians made off with the coveted "America's Cup," Newport had been the home of this much publicized race since its inception.

Next to boats and buildings, there is an abundance of wonderful seafood restaurants and bars in Newport. With Goat Island Marina, Bannister's Wharf, Christie's Dock, Newport Offshore, Treadway Marina, Newport Yachting Center (to name a few docks) and the large harbor, there are plenty of parking spaces.

Northeast Harbor is a busy and beautiful enclosed bay and resort town, with all the shoreside attractions. It is usually the scene of an interesting variety of craft. This is the point of embarkation for Mount Cadillac, the highest point on the Atlantic Coast.

Bass Harbor and Great Cranberry Island are rustic fishing ports with a stronger emphasis on fish and lobster than tour boats. Spurling Cove on Cranberry Island is a good launch for Schoodic and points east. Out in the fog and the Fundy tides is Roque Island, a wonderful reward after the ardors of the trip. The island is renowned for its quintessential white sand beach and swimmable water. It is privately owned by the Gardners, who invite sailors to enjoy and respect their environment.

A. South Bristol, Maine
B. S/V Edna, Vinalhaven, Maine
C. Stonington, Deer Isle, Maine

It has been claimed that no East Coast cruising man has been "Down East" until he has left the summer colonies of Mt. Desert behind, cleared Schoodic Head and plunged into the fog past Petit Manan Island. Unseen pleasures lie ahead then. The best of all, for me, is twenty-two miles ahead – Roque Island.

Solely-owned by the Gardner family, and wonderfully underpopulated, Roque is roughly a circular collection of a half-dozen islands of all sizes, cut by passages that form a lagoon about three-quarters of a mile in diameter. Its northern shore is a long half-moon beach of pure white sand – a South Seas effect nearly unique on Maine's rocky coast. It caused me to violate a lifelong promise to myself: never swim in Maine. The northeast shoreline is a high, wooded bluff that invites exploration. Anchorages abound – close to the beach, under the bluff, or off the western shore where there is a thoroughfare leading to the sort of creeks and small islands that will make you wish you had brought a sailing dinghy. All of this is wild, clean, untrammelled and protected from weather from any direction. If you wander far enough on foot to the north you will find the Gardner's enclave, but that is all. There are no facilities whatsoever. Bring your own – and make sure your Loran is working well. This is Down East.

Eric P. Swenson

Eric Swenson
Yachtsman/ Vice Chairman, W.W. Norton & Co.

A.

DANA JINKINS

DANA JINKINS

B.

C.

LYNN KARLIN

RICHARD BRISTOL

A.

BAY OF FUNDY

The radical tides of the Bay of Fundy constitute some formidable obstacles to navigating. They also provide vistas of savage beauty and a rich ecosystem. Grand Manan is a large Fundy island whose waters abound with seafood, and whose skies are filled with bird life. The Rockefellers designated nearby Kent Island as a wildlife sanctuary and bequeathed it to Bowdoin College of Maine.

Seal Cove and Grand Harbor on Grand Manan are friendly fishing ports with weathered charm, hearty fishermen and stout boats. A number of Fundy fishermen also build fish weirs which dry completely at low tide. Fisherman Gerald Lewis of Five Islands in the northern bay drives his horse and wagon out twice a day during low tide to collect the catch from his weir. It is labor-intensive — the weir must be rewoven with saplings each spring after the ice takes it out.

Farther down the Bay of Fundy the tidal currents are cumbersome enough to discourage many pleasure sailors. However, many yachtsmen have braved the commercial port of St. John, the Reversing Falls and fog in order to reach the gentle weather and bucolic shores of the St. John River.

Tradition has it that sailors, when ready to retire from the sea, shoulder an oar and head inland. When someone finally asks them what that wooden shovel is that they are carrying, they know they have put enough distance between themselves and the sea, and there they settle.

I got my foretaste of retirement from the seafaring life when I cruised to St. John, New Brunswick, through the justly renowned Reversing Falls, and up the St. John River as far as our draft would carry. This is a mecca for serious cruising sailors, and deservedly so. The contrasts were startling: the morning spent sailing down (up to landlubbers) the Bay of Fundy; lunch, a nervous gulped-and-not-tasted sandwich as we negotiated the Falls; and the afternoon a spinnaker-run up the St. John River amidst rolling farmland, feeling as if we had pulled a fast one on tradition and had successfully managed to head for our sailors' rest under full sail.

Leave the brown cows to starboard and the black cows to port say those in the know. We did, and were rewarded. In an unnamed cove in an uncharted lake we were granted one of those moments that we should not dare ask for, just gracefully accept. No moon, total blackness in absolute stillness, the reflected stars blending with the real ones at the horizon, the boat seemingly suspended in space. Then, for good measure, a display of northern lights. A loon calling was our anchor to earth.

I retired from active sailing years later, not surprisingly in a more prosaic fashion. That glimpse into one sailor's "aldila" made it easy.

Sandro Vitelli
Musician/ Scholar/ Navigator

The phenomenon of the Reversing Falls occurs at a ledge where the river spills into the harbor at low tide. What makes this tricky is the tide rises above the ledge and river level and starts flowing upriver. It is incumbent upon vessels to wait out the tide and sprint through the falls at slack water. If carefully negotiated, this maneuver is not as foolhardy as it sounds, and the rewards are superlative.

A. Lunenburg, Nova Scotia
B. St. John, New Brunswick
C. Peggy's Cove, Nova Scotia
D. Percé Rock, Gaspé Peninsula

NOVA SCOTIA

The distinctive character of Nova Scotia's innumerable harbors of enchantment is colored by the Grand Banks fisheries which they have served and sheltered. Well into the 20th century, Nova Scotia and New England fishing schooners competed for the hard-won providence of the Banks, thus creating the tradition of racing home from the fishing grounds. Shipwrights to the cod-fishing trade gradually refined their craft. The resultant fishing schooners evolved into fast and handsome vessels such as the *Bluenose* that adorns the Canadian dime.

The watery labyrinth of coast from Port Medway through Lunenburg and Mahone Bay to Peggy's Cove is a region of rich maritime history and harbors filled with handsome craft.

Lunenburg, where the schooner *Bluenose* was built, is the most fabled of these ports, and it is still enchanting. The red buildings that line the wharves house the equipment of a diversified fishing industry, in addition to several shipyards. Behind them historic dwellings, inns, shops and churches climb up a steep hill and down to the Back Harbor.

Far out on First Peninsula is the boatyard of David Stevens who has retired four or five times before going on to build one last, highly-prized yacht. Fine craftsmen still abound in Lunenburg. For instance, Mr. Dauphinée runs a rigging shop where he fashions beautiful wooden blocks, deadeyes and sundry gear and rigging to furnish traditional vessels.

Several active fishing and scallop fleets as well as a constant stream of yachts come and go from Lunenburg. The town has many renowned boatbuilders, a sail loft, a foundry and a working blacksmithy. Lunenburg scallops are out of this world.

The arduous technique of dory fishing from the "saltbanker" schooners in the brutally cold and stormy North Atlantic has ceased, but a strong fishing tradition lives on. It is well-chronicled in informative exhibits at the Fisheries Museum of the Atlantic.

THOMAS KAUL

B. C.

THOMAS KAUL

D.

THOMAS KAUL

NED GILLETTE

A.

B.

DEPT OF REG'L INDUSTRIAL EXPANSION PHOTO

HALIFAX

Halifax, one of the finest natural harbors in the world, is a cosmopolitan city, a trend which started with the influx of Loyalists following the American Revolutionary War. It is large and ice-free year-round; and has been an active shipbuilding port for years. It has served as a staging area for Allied naval fleets in both World Wars.

The inner harbor is primarily a recreational waterfront where a variety of craft, including the schooner *Bluenose II*, embark passengers from the renovated Historic Properties. The Northwest Arm of the harbor wends through park and residential districts and shelters legions of yachts. Nova Scotians are avid and far-ranging sailors who appreciate their own shores.

Nova Scotia has been compared to a lobster — girt with claws and carapace — but once you maneuver into the inside, it's "some good." It's true the coast is rocky, and fog can make it treacherous, but all dangers are well-charted. You can put into places with names like Ecum Secum or Antigonish or Liscomb Harbor or Ile Madame, and discover that each has a distinct cultural heritage, which is the real reward of a Nova Scotia cruise.

Halfway up the outer coast of Nova Scotia near Ecum Secum and Necum Teuch is Port Mouton. This is the only harbor Down East that has a sandy beach that reminds me of the Bahamas. When you drop your hook, the bottom is so clear that you can see your anchor 25 feet down. Any notion of the tropics is soon dispelled when you put your foot in the icy waters. When I sailed into the harbor and tied up alongside, the townspeople acted as if we were the first crusing vessel to visit in years. Everyone was extremely friendly and one gentleman took us shopping and showed us around. I have the distinct pleasure of being one of the five members of the Port Mouton Yacht Club.

Elizabeth Meyer
Author/ Owner of J Boat *Endeavor*

A. Bras d'Or Lakes
B. Halifax, Nova Scotia
C. Quebec City
D. Bonavista Bay, Newfoundland
E. Taddoussac Harbor

CAPE BRETON

The Bras d'Or Lakes, the salt-water interior of Cape Breton, offer magnificent cruising and a cultural feast. This entrancing northern island of Nova Scotia has a marvelous Old World feeling, with a strong presence of Scots, Gaelic and French-Acadian communities. I combined a charter cruise on the protected Bras d'Or Lakes with an overland tour, including the French village at Louisbourg, where a fiddling festival was in progress. The breathtaking scenic highway is called the Cabot Trail.

ST. LAWRENCE

It's not unusual for whales to congregate near the pretty harbor of Tadoussac, at the juncture of the Saguenay and the Saint Lawrence rivers. This area is remote and ruggedly beautiful, and becomes even more so across the river in the Gaspé Peninsula. The fishing ports in the St. Lawrence are historic and picturesque, and have good facilities for pleasure vessels.

Quebec City is a major inland seaport and an extraordinary haven for yachtsmen. The Château Frontenac crowns a promontory high above the river, where narrow streets perambulate a section of historic charm and festivity. The Old Town boasts gracious architecture and superb cuisine.

We could carry on into Montreal, Lake Champlain, or the St. Lawrence Seaway and continue on through the Great Lakes to Duluth or New Orleans. Harbors of enchantment abound in the inland waterways of this continent, too, from the silent purity of Georgian Bay to the healthy clamor of whistles and barges on the Mississippi. That will have to be another story.

Scenery and culture change around the world from port to port. But one thing remains the same, for the sojourner, the spectator, and the sailor alike; there is magic down by the waterfront — portents and possibilities and passages to anywhere. Harbors are the portals to the whole world, the doorways from a civilized, domestic, ordered life out into physical dangers, beauties, and the unknown.

DEPT OF REG'L INDUSTRIAL EXPANSION PHOTO

C. D.

DEPT OF REG'L INDUSTRIAL EXPANSION PHOTO

E.

CYNTHIA KAUL

Dana Jinkins, a photographer, artist and graphic designer, has co-authored three books: "Classic Yacht Interiors," "The World's Most Extradinary Yachts," and "St. Vincent and the Grenadines." Her yachting photographs have appeared in numerous publications world-wide. She is a partner in Concepts Publishing and is Art Director of this book. Dana spent many years living and sailing in the West Indies before settling in Vermont.

Rick Maloof, born in Boston, is owner and director of Audio Visual Productions, located just outside Salisbury, Maryland. He has been interested in photography since seventh grade. After high school, he joined the U.S. Army, attending various photography workshops until he retired in 1983. He has taught a color-slide workshop at the Art Institute and Gallery in Salisbury, Md., and has had a one man show at Artworks Gallery in Berlin, Md. Rick currently resides along the Wicomico River near Quantico, Maryland with his wife Joan, and daughter Alyssa.

Frank Piazza has always had a keen interest in photography. With a background in Architecture and Urban Planning from Columbia University, quality of life and environment have always been a high priority. His ability to combine his various interests in real estate investing, skiing and sailing gives him the opportunity to travel and photograph in foreign places. Frank lives in Moretown, Vermont.

Jeanette Phillipps is an architectural designer and freelance photographer from New York. Her photographs cover four Atlantic crossings and extensive cruising with husband Peter aboard their 50-foot Alden schooner, *Voyager*. Her work has appeared in "Wooden Boat" magazine and "The Seven Seas" calendar. She enjoys the compatibility of sailing, photography and architecture.

Stephanie Berke was born in Dublin, Ireland in 1944. She spent her childhood in the Sudan and Kenya. She organized luxury safaris in Kenya, Uganda and Tanzania from 1965 to 1972. Director of Tourism in the Seychelles Islands from 1973 to 1977, she then moved to the Caribbean as Tourism Adviser for the British Government. With two partners, Berke built and ran a hotel in Anguilla. She and her husband Norman embarked on the Yacht *Shirley B* for a round-the-world voyage in 1984 which took three-and-a-half years. She currently lives in London and Florida, and is working on a book and writing travel articles.

Hal Roth began sailing in 1962 and has made four long voyages: once around the Pacific from California to Japan, a second from California to New England via Cape Horn, plus two circumnavigations. All were made with his wife Margaret except his recent solo round-the-world voyage in S/Y *American Flag* in the BOC single-handed race. He is the author of seven books, all illustrated with his photographs. His sailing logbooks show 145,000 miles.

Neil Rabinowitz began photographing as a child. He earned a degree in journalism and has circumnavigated the world several times on a variety of cruising yachts, maxi-racers and oceanographic vessels, gaining a world-wide reputation as a marine photographer. His assignments topics range from the Olympics to the Indy-500, from the mountain tribes of Thailand to Alaskan glaciers. Neil currently resides on a small farm in Bainbridge Island, Washington.

Alison C. Langley, a freelance photographer since 1982, has spent three years sailing throughout the North and South Pacific as crew, cook and sailing instructor on *Eye of the Wind* (a square-rigged brigantine); *Show Me* (a Swan 651); and *Time* (a Swan 57).

She worked in film animation and special effects for several years and teaches sailboarding in Sydney, Australia, where she resides — when not at sea.

Werner Braun was born June 12th, 1918 in Nuremberg, Germany. He started his career as a freelance photographer when he emigrated to Israel in 1946. He became a recognized press photographer during the War of Independence and the Six-day War.

Twenty books of his photographs have been published and his pictures have appeared in hundreds of miscellaneous books, travel guides, magazines, posters, and encyclopedias all over the world. Braun is married to author Anat Rotem.

Roe Anne White, a native of California cruised with her husband for five years aboard their 31' foot gaff cutter, *Foye*, built in Fowey, England in 1904. They sailed around the Mediterranean for several years before sailing across the Atlantic, the Caribbean, through Panama and up the Pacific Coast to California. Roe Anne operates out of her photography studio, White Lightning. She resides in Santa Barbara with her son. Her recent works focus on portraiture.

Kelvin Jones is a British photojournalist based in Santa Monica, California. His work has been published world-wide in books and periodicals that include The London Sunday Times, Travel and Holiday, Time and Newsweek. His travel library covers the Middle and Far East, the Caribbean, and North and Central Americas. His photographs of Indonesia and Thailand are part of a major study on the Far East that is in process.

William (Bill) Robinson, is an editor, photographer, sailing aficianado, and author of enough books on sailing to create a library. His most recent books are "Caribbean Cruising Handbook" and "Eighty Years of Yachting." Formerly an editor at "Yachting Magazine" (1979-86), he is currently an editor-at-large at "Cruising World Magazine" and "Sailing World Magazine." He and his wife Jane reside in Rumson, New Jersey.

Nicola Dent, a native of the United Kingdom, and her husband Peter, sailed aboard the Baltic trader *Lene Marie* — she was the cook — for six years. During their world circumnavigation, they visited countless ports in over 30 countries. They currently reside in Pembrouceshire by the coast, and are renovating an old Welsh farmhouse.